Also by Martin Zweig
with Morrie Goldfischer

MARTIN ZWEIG'S
WINNING ON WALL STREET

MARTIN ZWEIG'S
WINNING WITH NEW
IRAs

MARTIN ZWEIG'S
WINNING WITH NEW IRAs

By Martin E. Zweig

With Morrie Goldfischer

WARNER BOOKS

A Warner Communications Company

W A Warner Communications Company

Printed in the United States of America

First Printing: February 1987

10 9 8 7 6 5 4 3 2 1

Library of Congress Cataloging in Publication Data

Zweig, Martin E.
  Martin Zweig's winning with new IRAs.

  Includes index.
  1. Individual retirement accounts. 2. Investments.
3. Stocks. I. Goldfischer, Morrie. II. Title.
HG1660.A3Z94 1987   332.024'01   86-28203
ISBN 0-446-51276-1

Book design: H. Roberts

To my mom and Mollie, Zack, Alex, and Dottie.

ACKNOWLEDGMENTS

I'd like to thank several people who helped make this book possible: Joan Graff and Lisa Liss, who typed the drafts; Jim Frost, Larry Kirshbaum, and everyone else at Warner Books; Nat Sobel, my agent; Ned Davis, Loren Flath, and Debbie Drake of Ned Davis Research, who created the Bond Timing Model and the graphics; and, of course, Morrie Goldfischer, my friend and collaborator.

CONTENTS

INTRODUCTION

IRAs—Still Your Best Retirement-Funding Bet

By now you have been bombarded with information and disinformation about the effects of the 1986 tax law on individual retirement accounts (IRAs). You have also been wooed by banks, brokerage houses, mutual funds, insurance companies, and others who are desperately eager to get their hands on your IRAs. If these diverse analyses and promises confuse you, it's understandable and you're in good company.

I've written *Winning with New IRAs* to guide you through the jungle of conflicting claims and to chart what I consider the best possible ways to invest in your IRA. I recommend the same strategy I use for many investors who have entrusted their funds to my management. To illustrate my methods, I present statistical and graphical information demonstrating that my techniques are safe and my results superior.

First, I want to emphasize that, despite any negative comments you may have read about the limitations imposed by the 1986 tax law, IRAs are still your best tax break even if you're not eligible for tax-deductible contributions. According to the Institute for Econometric Research, "IRAs remain an essential tax-planning device for all working people."

If you are among the millions of IRA investors not affected by the 1986 tax law (you'll find the current IRA regulations summarized in Chapter 4), it certainly is to your benefit to continue socking away $2,000 tax-deductible each year, investing the money wisely, and watching your nest egg grow.

Although the past is not necessarily prologue, my investment strategy described here has yielded a 17 percent return over a twenty-one-year period. If you invest $2,000 annually over thirty-five years and attain that rate of growth, your retirement bankroll will amount to over $3 million! (Tables 2–5 on pages 12–18 will show how you profit from different rates of return.)

So there's no question that, if the IRA rule changes haven't affected your eligibility, you should take advantage of your tax-deduction privileges.

Let's take the next group of IRA holders—those whose income limits them to smaller tax-deductible annual contributions. Even if your maximum IRA set-aside is restricted to $1,500, $1,000, or even $500, annual contributions are still in your best interest. Although the size of your retirement fund naturally will reflect the smaller investments, your holdings at the end of thirty or thirty-five years will be quite substantial—and you will be a lot better off by saving for the proverbial rainy day under the IRA umbrella.

Now, what if the new IRA ground rules prevent you from being a player with tax-deductible gains for your contributions. Is it still good economic sense for you to contribute 2,000 after-tax dollars and have your investment grow tax-deferred? The answer is an emphatic yes!

It's a matter of simple arithmetic. If you are in the 35 percent bracket (assuming 28 percent federal tax and 7 percent state and city taxes) and invest $2,000 after-tax annually at a 12 percent return, your tax shelter after thirty years would top a similar non-IRA investment by $200,000. (You'll find the explanatory figures in Table 6A on page 29.)

Considering other circumstances, let's suppose you and your spouse have accumulated $30,000 in your IRAs, are no longer eligible for tax-deductible contributions, and don't wish to make further investments that are merely tax-deferred. What should you do? Well, I strongly recommend that you leave your money in the IRAs and let them grow tax-sheltered. If you don't touch your $30,000 IRA and make no further contributions, here's how it will grow at various rates of return over thirty years:

10%..............................$ 523,482
12%.............................. 898,798
17%.............................. 3,331,940

In twenty years your $30,000 investment will increase as follows:

10%.............................$201,825
12%............................. 289,389
17%............................. 693,168

The tax-shelter aspect of IRAs can be especially valuable for rollovers of company pension funds. Under the 1986 tax law, you can only forward-average a lump-sum payout over five years instead of ten. This can lead to a much bigger tax bite that you can defer by rolling over the payment into an IRA. The investment then grows tax-deferred and, if you withdraw funds after you retire, your tax rate presumably will be lower.

THE BEST WAY TO MAKE A MILLION

Another dramatic illustration of how an IRA benefits from long-term tax-deferred compounding of earnings is provided by the Institute for Econometric Research. The institute compares two hypothetical individuals: Investor A who, starting at age nineteen, contributes $2,000 annually for just

HOW EARLY-AGE CONTRIBUTIONS
BOOST IRA INVESTMENTS

Age	INVESTOR A		INVESTOR B	
	IRA Contribution	Year-end Value	IRA Contribution	Year-end Value
19	$2,000	$ 2,200	0	0
20	2,000	4,620	0	0
21	2,000	7,282	0	0
22	2,000	10,210	0	0
23	2,000	13,431	0	0
24	2,000	16,974	0	0
25	2,000	20,872	0	0
26	2,000	25,159	0	0
27	0	27,675	$2,000	$ 2,200
28	0	30,442	2,000	4,620
29	0	33,487	2,000	7,282
30	0	36,835	2,000	10,210
31	0	40,519	2,000	13,431
32	0	44,571	2,000	16,974
33	0	49,028	2,000	20,872
34	0	53,930	2,000	25,159
35	0	59,323	2,000	29,875
36	0	65,256	2,000	35,062
37	0	71,781	2,000	40,769
38	0	78,960	2,000	47,045
39	0	86,856	2,000	53,950
40	0	95,541	2,000	61,545
41	0	105,095	2,000	69,899
42	0	115,605	2,000	79,089
43	0	127,165	2,000	89,198
44	0	139,882	2,000	100,318
45	0	153,870	2,000	112,550
46	0	169,257	2,000	126,005
47	0	186,183	2,000	140,805
48	0	204,801	2,000	157,086
49	0	225,281	2,000	174,995
50	0	247,809	2,000	194,694
51	0	272,590	2,000	216,364
52	0	299,849	2,000	240,200

CONTINUED

	INVESTOR A		INVESTOR B	
Age	IRA Contribution	Year-end Value	IRA Contribution	Year-end Value
53	0	$329,834	$2,000	$266,420
54	0	362,817	2,000	295,262
55	0	399,099	2,000	326,988
56	0	439,009	2,000	361,887
57	0	482,910	2,000	400,276
58	0	531,201	2,000	442,503
59	0	584,321	2,000	488,953
60	0	642,753	2,000	540,049
61	0	707,028	2,000	596,254
62	0	777,731	2,000	658,079
63	0	855,504	2,000	726,087
64	0	941,054	2,000	800,896
65	0	1,035,160	2,000	883,185
Less Total Invested		(16,000)		(78,000)
Net Earnings		$1,019,160		$805,185
Money Grew		64-fold		11-fold

Source: Institute for Econometric Research, 3471 North Federal Highway, Fort Lauderdale, Florida 33306

eight years and leaves his money untouched, and Investor B who begins his IRA at age twenty-seven and contributes $2,000 annually for thirty-nine years until age sixty-five.

Assuming both individuals earn 10 percent annually on their investments, who will wind up richer: the taxpayer who contributed $16,000 in earlier years or the one who set aside $78,000 in later years? The answer may surprise you.

As you'll see in the accompanying table, Investor A, who contributed $16,000, will see his investment grow to over $1 million at age sixty-five while Investor B will have considerably less despite having contributed nearly five times as much. The Institute for Econometric Research concludes:

"Clearly, when it comes to IRA contributions, sooner *is* better."

Summing up, regardless of your age, pension status, or income category, your IRA should play an important part in your retirement planning. And, if you follow the investment strategy I recommend for stock and bond trading, your winnings with IRAs can be a major factor in providing a secure financial future and the peace of mind that goes with it.

CHAPTER 1

The Explosive IRA Impact— Fun with Numbers

Before discussing the nitty-gritty of individual retirement accounts and how best to invest them, let's have a little fun with numbers by considering the future explosive impact of IRAs on our national economy.

I suspect hardly anyone has seriously considered the potentially gargantuan size of cumulative IRAs just a few decades from now, even with the 1986 tax law limitations. Remember, the majority of taxpayers are unaffected by the changes. Taxpayers allowed only partially deductible contributions can phase in nondeductible amounts to total $2,000 annually. And everyone not eligible for tax deductions can still put $2,000 each year into an IRA that will grow tax-deferred, a powerful incentive for regular investments. Although I can't forecast the precise future of IRAs, I'd like to fool around with a few figures to explore the possible consequences.

Currently, there are more than 40 million IRAs, although the present plan is only about six years old. An estimated 32 percent of all U.S. households now carry IRAs and undoubtedly the number of accounts will continue to climb. Some of the accounts are now owned by relatively older workers, say in their fifties or sixties, who will be pulling out money over the next decade or two. But many other accounts will be opened by people in their twenties and thirties or even early forties, who'll leave that money in for the next two, three, or even four decades.

For the purpose of this exercise, we'll forget completely about the approximately $230 billion now in IRAs. I'll assume that eventually 50 million accounts are opened and that contributions will be made to them for an average period of thirty years. Actually, the typical worker will probably work for about forty years, from his mid-twenties to mid-sixties at retirement. However, the youngest workers might have trouble setting aside the $2,000 maximum contribution. Moreover, if I use the forty-year time horizon in the examples that follow, the numbers would become absolutely unbelievable.

So let's suppose that roughly thirty years from now there will be in place 50 million IRAs, which have been growing via $2,000 annual contributions. This is an average figure that allows for millions of accounts that will have had shorter time frames and withdrawals, but includes many more newer accounts that might be funded for only five, ten, or fifteen years by the year 2017—thirty years down the road.

Now, I will show you later in the book how, with judicious trading in the stock market, you could make 12 to 17 percent per year in an IRA. Let's just use the lower number for now, 12 percent. That figure is also one which has been bandied about in many advertisements as a come-on for various mutual funds, zero coupon bonds, Ginnie Maes, and other investments. For most people, 12 percent doesn't seem that high, so let's try it out.

If you contribute $2,000 per year to an IRA for thirty years and compound that account at 12 percent, you will wind up with approximately $540,000 in thirty years. If 50 million investors do the same, the total value of those IRAs thirty years down the road would be a staggering $27 trillion. Just how big is that number?

Well, let's compare it to a crude estimate of gross national product. GNP now is roughly $3 trillion. Let's assume that GNP grows at 6 percent a year for the next thirty years. Three percentage points of that will be the assumed inflation rate, which is approximately the inflation rate of the past sixty years; the remaining three percentage points will be "real growth."

At a 6 percent growth rate, GNP in the year 2017 would be approximately $17.2 trillion. In other words, under these assumptions, the total funds in IRAs would be more than $9 trillion greater than estimated gross national product, thus topping the GNP by about 57 percent. Theoretically, it's possible for all IRA investments to exceed GNP because IRAs represent a balance-sheet-type item, or a lump sum, whereas GNP represents more of an income-statement-type figure, something which accrues over the course of a year. Nonetheless, for any economic number to top GNP, it is, indeed, a whopper.

Of course, it's highly unlikely—indeed, nearly impossible—for 50 million investors to achieve a 12 percent long-run rate of return in an economy where the assumed inflation rate will be 3 percent. However, suppose only 20 percent of all IRA investors opt to put their money into the stock market, a sum of 10 million assumed IRAs. Ten million stock investors earning 12 percent a year in IRAs, with $2,000 a year contributions, would accumulate $5.4 trillion in thirty years. That alone would equal about 31 percent of the estimated gross national product. But it would also represent an even larger proportion of the estimated value of the U.S. stock market.

Currently, the total value of stocks in the United States is about $2.3 trillion. Over the past sixty years, the stock market has produced a total return of 9.8 percent per year. Let's round it off and call it 10 percent. Roughly half of that, or 5 percent, came from dividends, the rest from capital appreciation. Let's assume that 10 percent total returns are produced by the stock market for the next thirty years; 5

percent of those returns will come from dividends, leaving only 5 percent for assumed future appreciation. If the $2.3 trillion of current stock were to appreciate at 5 percent for the next thirty years, the ending sum would equal $9.9 trillion.

The dividend payments are assumed a "leak" from the market. Of course, some people will reinvest their dividends, which is one reason why stocks would enjoy the 5 percent appreciation, as the dividend reinvestment demand helps to drive prices higher. If there are no other net additions or deletions on balance, stocks credited to IRAs will account for $5.4 of the $9.9 trillion of assumed stock market value in 2017, or an astounding 55 percent of the stock market. That is a much higher percentage than the current proportion of all institutional holdings in the stock market today.

Of course, you could argue that 10 million investors wouldn't be able to achieve the 12 percent return if the market as a whole earned only 10 percent. Agreed. So let's suppose that our 10 million IRA investors (20 percent of all IRA investors) go into the stock market and earn a return merely equal to that of the market as a whole, namely 10 percent. But remember, the IRA investor is going to retain his dividends in his account and reinvest them in stocks. So the IRA accounts will be growing at 10 percent a year, while the stock market as a whole will appreciate at only 5 percent a year.

Assuming $2,000 per year in contributions to the IRAs, a single account will grow to about $362,000 in thirty years, so 10 million accounts will grow to $3.6 trillion, or about 36 percent of the value of the stock market. Alternatively, let's assume that just over half of IRA investors decide to go into the stock market. If 27.3 million IRA accounts (55 percent of the assumed number of accounts) enter the stock market and earn that 10 percent per annum, the value of those accounts in thirty years would equal the $9.9 trillion valuation of the stock market.

Obviously, that's an absurdity. There would be zero market value left for all other individual holders of stocks and institutions. Something has to give. Perhaps nowhere near the number of IRA Investors will opt for stocks. Perhaps institutions, which now dominate that stock market, will become net liquidators of stocks. Perhaps individual owners will become net liquidators. Possibly a lot of new stock will be issued over the next thirty years, thereby increasing the total value of stocks.

But one thing is certain: The total value of stocks in IRAs cannot possibly exceed the total value of the stock market. Yet, if just over half of all IRA investors put their money into stocks and do no better or no worse than the market's total return, then, in thirty years, stock in IRAs would equal the value of the stock market.

One could contend that with so much new stock market money being invested in IRAs, it would prompt corporate America to issue new stock to willing buyers, thereby markedly increasing total outstanding value of common stocks. Indeed, in most past years, there has been a net addition to common stocks. That is, more new stock is generally issued during the course of the year than is retired by corporate and other buyouts.

However, in two recent years, 1984 and 1985, a very unusual development took place. Approximately $160 billion of common stock was removed on balance from the marketplace, even after adjusting for all new corporate stock. The stock was taken off the market through buyout activity, mostly from corporations themselves, either buying back their own stock or acquiring the stock of other corporations.

This pace, of course, could not continue indefinitely because it would eventually leave no stock around whatsoever. In fact, it is likely that at some point there will be net additions to stock outstanding rather than continued deletions

TABLE 1

THEORETICAL GROWTH OF STOCK IRAs
NEXT 30 YEARS
(Millions of IRAs in stocks and values in 30 years)
(In trillions of dollars)

1	2	3	4	5	6
ASSUMED RATES OF RETURN				**5 MILLION**	
Total Return	Div. Only	Apprec. Only	Market Value All Stock in 30 Years	Value Stock IRAs	% of All IRAs
10%	5%	5%	$9.94	$1.81	18%
9	5	4	7.46	1.49	20
8	5	3	5.58	1.23	22
7	5	2	4.17	1.01	24
6	5	1	3.10	0.84	27
5	5	0	2.30	0.70	30

like those of the past couple of years. But to keep things simple in this example, let's assume that there is no net change to stock outstanding.

Now glance at Table 1. The first column assumes six different annual rates of total return for stocks for the next thirty years ranging from 10 percent, roughly the norm of the past sixty years, down to just 5 percent. We'll assume in all cases that the dividend return is 5 percentage points of the total, seen in column 2. Column 3 shows the annual appreciation of stocks themselves, which is the total return of column 1 less the dividend return in column 2. In other words, 10 percent total return would be the sum of 5 percent in dividends and 5 percent appreciation. Or, for example, a 7 percent total return would equal 5 percentage points of dividends plus 2

7 8 10 MILLION		9 10 20 MILLION		11 12 30 MILLION	
Value Stock IRAs	% of All IRAs	Value Stock IRAs	% of All IRAs	Value Stock IRAs	% of All IRAs
$3.62	36%	$7.24	73%	$10.86	109%
2.97	40	5.94	80	8.91	119
2.45	44	4.90	88	7.35	132
2.02	48	4.04	97	6.06	145
1.68	54	3.36	108	5.04	163
1.40	61	2.80	122	4.20	183

percentage points of appreciation. Ironically, the IRA influence becomes more astonishing the poorer the market performs.

Column 4 shows the approximate market value of all stocks thirty years down the road, given the capital appreciation of column 3. Once again, I have supposed no additions or deletions of stock. Column 5 assumes that only 5 million IRAs, about 10 percent of all IRAs, go into the stock market. I'll assume in all cases that IRA investors earn the same total return achieved by the stock market. Thus in the first line of the table in column 5, we have supposed that 5 million IRA investors earn 10 percent per annum in thirty years. If so, they would wind up with a total of $1.81 trillion in the year 2017. That would equal (column 6) about 18 percent of the valuation of the stock market, a very significant proportion of the total. Yet, that is probably a too conservative estimate of what lies ahead.

Probably a fairer estimate would lie in the seventh column of the first line, where 10 million IRA investors would invest in stocks (20 percent of all IRA investors) and earn the market's long-run rate of return of 10 percent. That would produce a total value of $3.62 trillion in IRAs, or 36 percent of the total valuation of the stock market. In other words, I think it's not impossible—indeed, it is even likely—that IRA investors would control about one third of the valuation of the U.S. stock market in thirty years.

Keep going across the right on the first line to the next two columns, where we assume 20 million investors buy stocks (40 percent of all IRAs). That would produce a value of $7.24 trillion in thirty years, nearly three quarters of the value of the whole stock market. Finally, in the last two columns, I have assumed that 30 million IRA investors, or some 60 percent of all IRAs, go into the stock market and earn the market's rate of return. That would produce an incredible $10.86 trillion of market value, or some 109 percent of the assumed valuation of all common stocks. Obviously, that's an absurdity because it is impossible for one subset of investors to own more stock than there is stock!

If you think that sounds crazy, it gets even more ridiculous as we assume lower returns for the stock market on the whole. In line 2, where I have assumed 9 percent total return, or just 4 percent appreciation, the total market value of all stock in thirty years would be $7.46 trillion (column 4). If we then assume that 10 million IRA investors buy stock, they would wind up with $2.97 trillion, or 40 percent of the market value of stocks. That is within reason, but if 30 million IRA investors buy stock, they would end up with 119 percent of the total value of all stock!

The craziest number of all would be in the lower right-hand corner of the table where it is assumed that there is no appreciation in the stock market over the next thirty years but where dividends still return 5 percent per year. Again, assuming no net issuance of stock over that time, the market value would still be the same $2.3 trillion it is today. But if even 20 million IRA investors went into the stock market and kept plowing back their dividends, they would control $2.8 trillion of stock in thirty years, or 122 percent of the total. Thirty million IRA investors would end up with $4.2 trillion, or 183 percent of the stock market!

One can generate all sorts of absurd numbers using "logical" rates of return and "logical" percentages of IRA investors going into stocks. No matter what assumptions are used, the percentage of stock market value controlled by IRA investors a few decades down the road is going to be very substantial.

Of course, only a small percentage of IRA investors will go into stocks. But assume for argument's sake that IRA investors get very logical and shun short-term money market investments such as CDs and Treasury bills. After all, institutional pension investments keep only a very small fraction of their funds in such instruments. The overwhelming bulk of institutional pension money goes into stocks and bonds.

Let's pretend that IRA investors do likewise, and place one third of their money into the stock market and two thirds into the bond market. Let's also assume that the total rate of return in the stock market for the next thirty years is the approximate 10 percent that it has averaged over the last sixty years. We'll also assume that the government bond market produces a total return of 4 percent per annum over the next thirty years, just as it has done the last sixty years.

Using this one-third, two-thirds split, the total rate of return per annum in IRAs would equal 6 percent, or the same growth rate that I am assuming for gross national product. Thus, by the year 2016, GNP is assumed to be $9.9 trillion and the value of 50 million IRAs equals $8.4 trillion, or about 84 percent of total GNP. That, by the way, is not an absurdity. But it does mean that individual retirement accounts will become a very powerful factor in the U.S. economy. And it's another very good reason why you should be a member of that money-building IRA fraternity.

CHAPTER 2

The Million-Dollar Difference—If You Treat Your IRA Right

*L*et's start with a lesson in simple arithmetic.

If you put $2,000 a year into an individual retirement account (IRA) and earn a 10 percent annual return, you'll have amassed $361,887 at the end of thirty years. Not bad.

However, if you put that same $2,000 annually into an IRA at 17 percent interest, your nest egg will be worth $1,515,010 after thirty years. That's a lot better. Precisely $1,153,123 better.

I would like to show you how to achieve the greater sum. While there are no guarantees, the investment approach that I will recommend, describe in detail, and document, has attained the 17 percent result over a period of twenty-one years. And, since history has a way of repeating itself over the long run, it is not unreasonable to expect a return in the same ball park in the years ahead. All you have to do is read this book and invest fifteen minutes or so a week following my instructions on keeping track of two or three key market indicators.

Before we get into specifics, let's look at why the government encouraged the development of individual retirement accounts, better known as IRAs. There were two basic reasons. First, it wanted to encourage savings. This makes more funds available for investment in factories, equipment, and other areas that stimulate the economy. Second, it wanted to help individuals acquire a monetary cushion for their later years. Skeptics argue that the government questioned the ultimate vitality of the Social Security system and established IRAs as a fail-safe mechanism. But, regardless of the future of Social Security (and it seems structurally solvent until the end of this century), the IRAs certainly give people a tax-advantaged way to provide for what can truly be their golden years.

If you can afford it—and it would pay to skimp elsewhere if you have to—it is downright foolhardy not to have an IRA. You'll see why if you take a good look at Tables 2 through 5, which show how your IRA dollars can grow at different compound interest rates. A few random figures for $2,000 invested annually on the first of each year over a thirty-five-year period: at 6 percent—$236,241; at 10 percent—$596,254; at 12 percent—$966,927; at 17 percent—$3,337,990!

That's why over 40 million Americans have opened such accounts in the past six years. So far, so good. The problem,

TABLE 2

HOW YOUR IRA INVESTMENT INCREASES AT VARIOUS COMPOUND GROWTH RATES

(Assuming $2,000 investment on the first of each year)

Year	5%	6%	7%	8%	9%
1	$ 2,100	$ 2,120	$ 2,140	$ 2,160	$ 2,180
2	4,305	4,367	4,430	4,493	4,556
3	6,620	6,749	6,880	7,012	7,146
4	9,051	9,274	9,501	9,733	9,969
5	11,064	11,951	12,307	12,672	13,047
6	14,284	14,788	15,308	15,846	16,401
7	17,098	17,795	18,520	19,273	20,057
8	20,053	20,983	21,956	22,975	24,042

(TABLE 2 continued)

HOW YOUR IRA INVESTMENT INCREASES AT VARIOUS COMPOUND GROWTH RATES

(Assuming $2,000 investment on the first of each year)

Year	5%	6%	7%	8%	9%
9	23,156	24,362	25,633	26,973	28,386
10	26,414	27,943	29,567	31,291	33,121
11	29,834	31,740	33,777	35,954	38,281
12	33,426	35,764	38,381	40,991	43,907
13	37,197	40,030	43,101	46,430	50,038
14	41,157	44,552	48,258	52,304	56,722
15	45,315	49,345	53,776	58,649	64,007
16	49,681	54,426	59,681	65,501	71,947
17	54,265	59,811	65,998	72,901	80,603
18	59,078	65,520	72,758	80,893	90,037
19	64,132	71,571	79,991	89,524	100,320
20	69,439	77,985	8⁻,730	98,846	111,529
21	75,010	84,785	96,012	108,914	123,747
22	80,861	91,992	104,872	119,787	137,064
23	87,004	99,631	114,353	131,530	151,580
24	93,454	107,729	124,498	144,212	167,042
25	100,227	116,313	135,353	157,909	184,648
26	107,338	125,411	146,968	172,702	203,446
27	114,805	135,056	159,395	188,678	223,937
28	122,645	145,279	172,693	205,932	246,271
29	130,878	156,116	186,922	224,567	270,615
30	139,521	167,603	202,146	244,692	297,151
31	148,598	179,779	218,437	266,427	326,074
32	158,127	192,686	235,867	289,902	357,601
33	168,134	206,367	254,518	315,254	391,965
34	178,640	220,869	274,474	342,634	429,422
35	189,672	236,241	295,827	372,205	470,250
36	201,256	252,536	318,675	404,141	514,752
37	213,419	269,808	343,122	438,632	563,260
38	226,190	288,117	369,281	475,883	616,134
39	239,599	307,524	397,271	516,114	673,766
40	253,679	328,095	427,220	599,563	736,584

TABLE 3

HOW YOUR IRA INVESTMENT INCREASES AT VARIOUS COMPOUND GROWTH RATES

(Assuming $2,000 investment on the first of each year)

Year	10%	11%	12%	13%	14%
1	$ 2,200	$ 2,220	$ 2,240	$ 2,260	$ 2,280
2	4,620	4,684	4,749	4,814	4,879
3	7,282	7,419	7,559	7,700	7,842
4	10,210	10,456	10,706	10,961	11,220
5	13,431	13,826	14,230	14,645	15,071
6	16,974	17,567	18,178	18,809	19,461
7	20,872	21,719	22,599	23,515	24,466
8	25,159	26,328	27,551	28,831	30,171
9	29,875	31,444	33,098	34,840	36,675
10	35,062	37,123	39,309	41,629	44,089
11	40,769	43,426	46,266	49,300	52,542
12	47,045	50,423	54,058	57,969	62,177
13	53,950	58,190	62,785	67,765	73,162
14	61,545	66,811	72,559	78,835	85,685
15	69,900	76,380	83,507	91,344	99,961
16	79,089	87,002	95,767	105,478	116,235
17	89,198	98,792	109,499	121,450	134,788
18	100,318	111,879	124,879	139,499	155,938
19	112,550	126,406	142,105	159,894	180,050
20	126,005	142,530	161,937	182,940	207,537
21	140,806	160,429	183,005	208,982	238,872
22	157,086	180,296	207,206	238,410	274,594
23	174,995	202,438	234,311	271,663	315,317
24	194,694	226,827	264,668	309,239	361,742
25	216,364	253,998	298,668	351,700	414,665
26	240,200	284,157	336,748	399,681	474,999
27	266,420	317,635	379,398	453,900	543,778
28	295,262	354,795	427,166	515,167	622,187
29	326,988	396,042	480,666	584,398	711,573
30	361,887	441,827	540,585	662,630	813,474
31	400,276	492,647	607,696	751,032	929,640

(TABLE 3 continued)

HOW YOUR IRA INVESTMENT INCREASES AT VARIOUS COMPOUND GROWTH RATES
(Assuming $2,000 investment on the first of each year)

Year	10%	11%	12%	13%	14%
32	442,503	549,059	682,859	850,926	1,062,070
33	488,954	611,675	767,042	963,807	1,213,040
34	540,049	681,179	861,327	1,091,360	1,385,140
35	596,254	758,329	966,927	1,235,500	1,581,350
36	658,080	843,965	1,085,200	1,398,370	1,805,010
37	726,087	939,022	1,217,660	1,582,420	2,060,000
38	800,896	1,044,530	1,366,020	1,790,400	2,350,670
39	883,186	1,161,650	1,532,180	2,025,410	2,682,050
40	973,704	1,291,650	1,718,290	2,290,970	3,059,820

TABLE 4

HOW YOUR IRA INVESTMENT INCREASES AT VARIOUS COMPOUND GROWTH RATES
(Assuming $2,000 investment on the first of each year)

Year	15%	16%	17%	18%	19%
1	$ 2,300	$ 2,320	$ 2,340	$ 2,360	$ 2,380
2	4,945	5,011	5,078	5,145	5,212
3	7,987	8,133	8,281	8,431	8,583
4	11,485	11,754	12,029	12,308	12,593
5	15,508	15,955	16,414	16,884	17,366
6	20,134	20,828	21,544	22,283	23,045
7	25,454	26,480	27,547	28,654	29,804
8	31,572	33,037	34,569	36,172	37,847
9	38,607	40,643	42,786	45,043	47,418
10	46,699	49,466	52,400	55,510	58,807
11	56,003	59,700	63,648	67,862	72,361
12	66,704	71,572	76,808	82,437	88,489
13	79,009	85,344	92,205	99,636	107,682

(TABLE 4 continued)

HOW YOUR IRA INVESTMENT INCREASES AT VARIOUS COMPOUND GROWTH RATES

(Assuming $2,000 investment on the first of each year)

Year	15%	16%	17%	18%	19%
14	93,161	101,319	110,220	119,931	130,521
15	109,435	119,850	131,298	143,878	157,701
16	128,150	141,346	155,958	172,136	190,044
17	149,673	166,281	184,811	205,481	228,532
18	174,424	195,206	218,569	244,827	274,333
19	202,887	228,759	258,066	291,256	328,836
20	235,620	267,681	304,277	346,042	393,695
21	273,263	312,830	358,344	410,690	470,877
22	316,553	365,203	421,602	486,974	562,724
23	366,336	425,955	495,615	576,990	672,022
24	423,586	496,428	582,209	683,208	802,086
25	489,424	578,176	683,535	808,545	956,862
26	565,137	673,004	802,064	956,443	1,141,050
27	652,208	783,005	940,755	1,130,960	1,360,220
28	752,339	910,606	1,103,020	1,336,900	1,621,050
29	867,490	1,058,620	1,292,880	1,579,900	1,931,430
30	999,913	1,230,320	1,515,010	1,866,640	2,300,780
31	1,152,200	1,429,490	1,774,900	2,205,000	2,740,310
32	1,327,330	1,660,530	2,078,970	2,604,250	3,263,340
33	1,528,730	1,928,540	2,434,730	3,075,380	3,885,760
34	1,760,340	2,239,420	2,850,980	3,631,310	4,626,430
35	2,026,690	2,600,050	3,337,990	4,287,310	5,507,840
36	2,332,990	3,018,380	3,907,780	5,061,380	6,556,710
37	2,685,240	3,503,640	4,574,450	5,974,790	7,804,860
38	3,090,330	4,006,540	5,354,440	7,052,610	9,290,160
39	3,556,180	4,719,510	6,267,040	8,324,440	11,057,700
40	4,091,900	5,476,950	7,334,770	9,825,200	13,161,000

TABLE 5

HOW YOUR IRA INVESTMENT INCREASES AT VARIOUS COMPOUND GROWTH RATES
(Assuming $2,000 investment on the first of each year)

Year	20%	21%	22%	23%	24%
1	$ 2,400	$ 2,420	$ 2,440	$ 2,460	$ 2,480
2	5,280	5,348	5,417	5,486	5,555
3	8,736	8,891	9,049	9,208	9,368
4	12,883	13,179	13,479	13,785	14,097
5	17,860	18,366	18,885	19,416	19,960
6	23,832	24,643	25,479	26,342	27,231
7	30,998	32,238	33,525	34,860	36,246
8	39,598	41,428	43,340	45,338	47,425
9	49,917	52,548	55,315	58,226	61,287
10	62,301	66,003	69,924	74,078	78,476
11	77,161	82,283	87,747	93,575	99,790
12	94,993	101,983	109,492	117,558	126,220
13	116,392	125,819	136,020	147,056	158,992
14	142,070	154,661	168,384	183,339	199,630
15	172,884	189,560	207,869	227,967	250,022
16	209,861	231,787	256,040	282,859	312,507
17	254,233	282,883	314,809	350,377	389,988
18	307,480	344,708	386,507	433,423	486,066
19	371,376	419,517	473,979	535,571	605,201
20	448,052	510,036	580,694	661,212	752,930
21	540,062	619,563	710,887	815,751	936,113
22	650,474	752,091	869,722	1,005,830	1,163,260
23	782,969	912,451	1,063,500	1,239,640	1,444,920
24	941,963	1,106,490	1,299,910	1,527,210	1,794,180
25	1,132,760	1,341,270	1,588,330	1,880,930	2,227,270
26	1,361,710	1,625,350	1,940,200	2,316,000	2,764,290
27	1,636,450	1,969,100	2,369,490	2,851,150	3,430,200
28	1,966,140	2,385,030	2,893,220	3,509,370	4,255,930
29	2,361,770	2,888,300	3,532,160	4,318,980	5,279,830
30	2,836,520	3,497,270	4,311,680	5,314,810	6,549,470
31	3,406,220	4,234,110	5,262,690	6,539,680	8,123,830
32	4,089,870	5,125,700	6,422,920	8,046,260	10,076,000

(TABLE 5 continued)

HOW YOUR IRA INVESTMENT INCREASES AT VARIOUS COMPOUND GROWTH RATES
(Assuming $2,000 investment on the first of each year)

Year	20%	21%	22%	23%	24%
33	4,910,240	6,204,520	7,838,410	9,899,360	12,496,800
34	5,894,690	7,509,880	9,565,300	12,178,700	15,498,500
35	7,076,030	9,089,380	11,672,100	14,982,200	19,220,600
36	8,493,630	11,000,600	14,242,400	18,430,600	23,836,000
37	10,194,800	13,313,100	17,378,200	22,672,100	29,559,100
38	12,236,100	16,111,300	21,203,800	27,889,100	36,655,800
39	14,685,700	19,497,100	25,871,100	34,306,100	45,455,600
40	17,625,300	23,593,900	31,565,200	42,199,000	56,367,500

in my opinion, is that the bulk of the over $230 billion in IRA funds (at this writing) is invested in the wrong vehicles.

According to Market Facts, a Chicago-based research firm, an estimated 46 percent of IRA investments at year-end 1985 was in certificates of deposit, 7 percent in money market deposit accounts, and 6 percent in corporate stocks and bonds.

Mind you, I'm not saying that the huge investments in certificates of deposit and money market deposit accounts are risky; you're not going to lose your money in them. But the long-range returns on these interest-bearing accounts probably will be considerably less than you could earn in stocks or, for that matter, in bonds.

In preparing for retirement, most of you—certainly if you're in your mid-fifties or younger—have time working on your side. Although stocks are more volatile than savings accounts and CDs, eventually they will produce greater wealth . . . and that seems a laudable goal for retirement.

However, many people, unfamiliar with the stock market or having once been burned, are afraid of the risks associated with it. As a result, they have forgone the higher long-term returns available in stocks for the safer and more certain money market instruments. This bird-in-hand philosophy may give more peace of mind temporarily but will result in a lot less money for retirement.

History shows that the total returns on stocks, including both capital gains and dividend income, will soundly beat the returns on savings accounts and CDs—despite risks along the way of bear markets. In this book I will describe fully a method by which you can invest in equities—by way of no-load mutual funds—and eliminate the greater proportion of risk inherent with stock market downturns. By avoiding the declining periods in the stock market, you can wind up with more money at retirement than if you had simply bought stocks, salted them away, and forgot about them for many years.

If you're reading this book or thinking about reading it, you're entitled to know my qualifications for recommending how you invest your hard-earned retirement money. Naturally, I might be the most qualified person in the world but that wouldn't guarantee that my advice would be any good. So I'll let you judge whether I am qualified and then, of course, you'll be the judge on whether my advice is good, bad, or indifferent.

I've been involved in the stock market for twenty-five years, beginning when I was a freshman in college at the Wharton School at the University of Pennsylvania. I spent nine years in college studying finance, picking up an M.B.A. at the University of Miami and a Ph.D. in finance at Michigan State along the way. For fifteen years I was a college professor, teaching investments and corporation finance.

In 1971 I began publishing *The Zweig Forecast*, an advisory letter sold to thousands of subscribers. *The Zweig Forecast* gives predictions on the general course of the market and recommends individual stocks. Since mid-1980 the *Hulbert Financial Digest,* Washington, D.C., has been monitoring track records of the seventy-two major advisory services. For the six years through late June 1986, my *Zweig Forecast* was up 252 percent, including more than ample allowance for all commissions. Moreover, there were no down years, a statement that only three other services can make over that period. In two of those calendar years I was ranked the number one service.

For more than fourteen years I've been director of research to Avatar Associates, a firm which manages pension money for large corporations. We run several hundred million dollars. In 1981 I started a joint venture with Avatar called Zweig/Avatar Trend Timing Services, in which we manage money for individuals and smaller pension accounts. ZATTS, as it is called, does not invest in stocks directly. Rather, we purchase no-load mutual funds (which own stocks) when our indicators are bullish. And late in 1986 I launched The Zweig Fund, a closed-end mutual fund with more than $300 million in assets trading on the New York Stock Exchange.

Our ZATTS track record from inception in mid-1981 to the end of the first quarter of 1986 is 24.8 percent per year, which comes out to 187 percent compounded for the 4¾ years. That's about triple per annum what you could have earned in CDs or savings accounts and it's about four times better than the inflation rate. It's also about 6 percentage points a year better than you could have done by buying stocks and squirreling them away, the so-called buy-and-hold approach.

Because of the limited number of accounts that we can reasonably manage, our minimum account size is about $100,000. Unfortunately, that means there's no way we can cope with the typical IRA account, even though many of these holdings are becoming quite respectable in size. I wish we could accept IRA accounts of less than $100,000, but the economics of the business simply dictate that we can't. However, this book might be the next best thing. That's because I will describe here in detail my investment philosophies and strategies.

Now, I can't reproduce the exact indicators and models that I use to make investment decisions for The Zweig Fund, ZATTS, Avatar, or *The Zweig Forecast*. They would be far too complicated for the nonprofessional. However, I have developed simplified models which you, the individual investor, can follow with minimum hassle and by spending only a few minutes a week.

My easy-to-follow models will enable you to make solid long-run investment decisions that will help you beat the stock and bond markets over time, yet reduce your risk exposure considerably. You'll also find that trading no-load mutual funds is very simple, generally involving no more than a single telephone call. It's unsophisticated enough for a novice to do. You don't have to be an experienced investor to follow my strategies in this book.

Getting back to my qualifications, since 1970 I've been a regular contributor to *Barron's*, in which I've written a few dozen articles on market forecasting over the years. I've also been a regular on Public Television's *Wall Street Week with Louis Rukeyser* since 1973. Finally, I'm the author of *Martin Zweig's Winning on Wall Street*, published in 1986 by Warner Books, the same publisher of this book.

Winning on Wall Street gives specific indicators for tracking the direction of the stock market and then goes on to tell how to pick stocks and how to sell them. It was designed for the general investor who is interested in the stock market itself. I've decided to borrow and simplify some of the crucial information from *Winning on Wall Street* and concentrate on how the IRA investor can go about knowing when to buy and sell stock and bond mutual funds.

First, let's take a look at why it is so important to have an IRA and to treat it with the respect that it deserves.

CHAPTER 3

IRA—Your Key to Financial Security

*I*f you are concerned about your future retirement needs, the best financial advice I can give you at this time is to open and contribute annually to an IRA. That holds true even if current IRA regulations make you ineligible to salt away tax-deductible dollars.

Yes, if you are a working person with meaningful income and are paying federal income tax, an IRA is an investment opportunity you should not refuse. As proof, I will provide several numerical examples making assumptions about different income brackets and different rates of return on investment over a thirty-year period. I'll then show what you would wind up with after taxes with an IRA versus investing the same amount without an IRA.

During this part of the discussion, we'll assume that you are eligible to make tax-deductible contributions to an IRA. In the first example (as illustrated in Table 6), we'll start at the high end of the tax range, the 35 percent bracket. I've computed that figure by assuming a 28 percent federal tax and a 10 percent state and city tax. With 28 percent of the 10 percent deductible, the remainder is approximately 7 percent, which is added to the original 28 percent. (States to which this figure might apply include New York and California.)

TABLE 6

RESULTS OF IRA AND NON-IRA PROGRAMS AFTER 30 YEARS
(Assuming *deductible* $2,000 annual contribution)

	35% TAX BRACKET		15% TAX BRACKET	
	With IRA	Without IRA	With IRA	Without IRA
Gross Income	$ 2,000	$ 2,000	$ 2,000	$ 2,000
Less Income Tax	0	700	0	300
Available to Invest	$ 2,000	$ 1,300	$ 2,000	$ 1,700
Assumed Investment Rate	12%	12%	12%	12%
Less Tax of Investment Returns	0	4	0	2
Net Annual Earning Rate	12%	8%	12%	10%
Value of Account in 30 Years	$540,585	$159,050	$540,585	$307,604
Less Income Tax During Retirement Years	189,205	0	81,088	0
Net Amount	$351,380	$159,050	$459,497	$307,604
IRA Advantage	+$192,330		+$151,893	
Value of Account in 30 Years	$540,585	$159,050		
Less Income Tax in Retirement (more realistically assuming lower tax bracket of 20%)	108,117	0		
Net Amount	$432,468	$159,050		
IRA Advantage	+$273,418			

Let's assume this high bracket for the moment. Let's also suppose that you could get a fairly generous 12 percent per annum return on investment, be it stocks, bonds, or whatever, and that that figure would be the average return over a thirty-year span. Next, we will assume that you place $2,000 into your IRA each year over thirty years, a total investment of $60,000.

The obvious advantage of putting this money into an IRA is that you defer $2,000 from current taxes. If you're in the 35 percent bracket, this means a $700 income tax saving. If you were to take $2,000 of pretax ordinary income and invest it on your own (without an IRA), you would find that you would have only $1,300 left after taxes. So the IRA investor gets an edge over the non-IRA investor because, in the 35 percent bracket, he's able to put away more than one and one-half times as much money. Of course, the benefits are proportionately less in lower tax brackets.

There is a second advantage for the IRA investor. The earned interest, dividends, and capital gains are also deferred from taxes until he retires. This enables the IRA investor in this example to compound his returns at the projected 12 percent rate, without the leakage of taxes. The non-IRA investor must pay the tax on earnings as they accrue. Therefore, he cannot compound at the 12 percent rate. Interest and dividend income and capital gains would be taxed at the assumed 35 percent rate. If you were earning a 12 percent pretax return and had to pay out a third for taxes, the after-tax net would be only 7.8 percent, which I'll round to 8 percent for simplicity. So the IRA investor can compound at 12 percent, the non-IRA investor at only 8 percent.

The non-IRA investor has at least one advantage. At the end of thirty years, his income tax is fully paid up. All the money left is his. The IRA investor cannot say the same. IRAs don't let you avoid tax; they merely *defer* the tax until the money is taken out of the IRA. To make this example simple, let's make the rather unrealistic assumption that after thirty years the IRA investor withdrew all the money at once from his account. Consequently, he will pay ordinary income tax rates on that sum. In actuality, the IRA investor is more apt to take the money out slowly during his retirement, thus stretching the tax deferment over a longer period.

The amount of money is likely to be rather large, so that even in retirement let's assume that this fairly well off investor is still in the 35 percent tax bracket. Using tables for compounding returns, we would find that a $2,000 investment each year for thirty years, when compounded at 12 percent, becomes $541,000 in thirty years. (By the way, to keep the arithmetic as easy as possible, I am rounding all these numbers to the nearest thousand dollars, although Table 6 rounds to the nearest dollar.) So even though the IRA investor has a gross of $541,000 at the end of thirty years, if he pulls it all out at once, at the 35 percent rate, he will wind up with $351,000 after taxes.

Remember, the non-IRA investor in the 35 percent tax bracket has only $1,300 left to invest after a $2,000 pretax income. Uncle Sam and the state and city take away the other $700. Compounding that $1,300 at the 8 percent rate (again, after that 35 percent annual tax leakage) gives a final wealth of $159,000 in year thirty. That's less than half the $351,000 that the IRA investor will have achieved.

Naturally, the higher the tax bracket, the more the IRA investor is favored over the non-IRA investor. So let's take a second example using a more moderate tax bracket, but still sticking with an assumed investment return of 12 percent a year. Let's use a 15 percent income tax rate, which, under the new tax law, is the lowest. I've also assumed this time that there is no state income tax.

The IRA investor would keep putting away his $2,000 a year for thirty years, again winding up with $541,000 gross in year thirty. Assume that at retirement he still remains in the 15 percent bracket. Thus, he would retain 85 percent of that amount after paying the tax, or some $459,000.

What about the non-IRA investor? His interest and dividends over the thirty years would be taxed at the 15 percent rate. This would whittle down the pretax investment return of 12 percent a year to roughly 10 percent a year (before rounding, it's actually 10.2 percent), the penalty for tax leakage on the investment.

The non-IRA investor in the 15 percent bracket would pay $300 in taxes on $2,000 of pretax income, leaving him with $1,700 per year. Seventeen hundred dollars invested annually at a return of 10 percent (allowing that 2-percentage-point leakage for taxes along the way) compounds to an ending value of $308,000. That's a lot better than the 35 percent bracket non-IRA investor did in the earlier example, but it's still far less of an ending wealth than the IRA investor would receive in the 15 percent bracket. The former winds up with $459,000 and the non-IRA investor gets $308,000, an IRA advantage of $152,000! So we see that even in a low tax bracket, it definitely pays to have an IRA.

THE IRA $200,000 AFTER-TAX ADVANTAGE WITHOUT TAX-DEDUCTIBLE CONTRIBUTION

Is it still profitable under the new tax law to put money into an IRA even if your contribution is not tax-deductible? You bet it is. Let me show you why.

First, let's talk about tax rates. If you and your spouse together are earning over $50,000 (gross income) and either of you has a corporate pension plan, you are not eligible for the $2,000 tax-deductible annual IRA contribution.

That income implies that your tax rate is at least 28

percent, the highest of the two new brackets, and we're not even talking about that hump at 33 percent which kicks in between 15 and 28 percent, a gimmick that only Congress could figure out. So let's suppose you're in the 28 percent bracket and live where state and/or city taxes could lift you to 35 percent. (As in the illustration at the opening of this chapter, I reached the 35 percent rate by assuming a combined 10 percent state and city tax, 28 percent of which is deductible from your federal return, which adds about 7 percent to the 28 percent tax rate.)

Now we'll examine what happens to the person without the IRA. He's the reasonably wealthy individual (found in the right-hand column of Table 6A) who says, "What do I need an IRA for?" He's wrong. Here are the figures which should give him second thoughts.

Assuming that the non-IRA holder is in the 35 percent bracket, he'll need to earn $3,077 in pretax income to have $2,000 left after taxes. As in the earlier examples, let's suppose he can earn 12 percent on his money. The person without the IRA will be taxed 35 percent on his interest, dividends, and any future capital gains income. Remember, there are no more long-term capital gains. That means that over one third of his 12 percent will be taxed away. I've rounded it out and we'll say he retains about 8 percentage points of his 12 percent gain. Over thirty years, his $2,000 after-tax contribution compounded each year at 8 percent comes out to $245,000.

But our wiser upper-income IRA investor (first column in Table 6A) compounds at 12 percent each year. There is no tax leakage, and he winds up with $541,000. Unfortunately, the IRA holder does have to pay some taxes when he retires. For argument's sake, let's assume his tax rate will be 35 percent at retirement, a figure that may be awfully high for somebody at that stage in life.

He will not have to pay 35 percent on the entire $540,000 because $60,000 is his own after-tax contribution. So he really

TABLE 6A

RESULTS OF IRA AND NON-IRA PROGRAMS AFTER 30 YEARS
(Assuming *nondeductible* $2,000 annual contribution)

	35% TAX BRACKET	
	With IRA	Without IRA
Gross Income	$3,077	$3,077
Less Income Tax	1,077	1,077
Available to Invest	$2,000	$2,000
Assumed Investment Rate	12%	12%
Less Tax of Investment Returns	0	4
Net Annual Earning Rate	12%	8%
Value of Account in 30 Years	$540,585	$244,692
Less Income Tax During Retirement Years	168,205	0
Net Amount	$372,380	$244,692
IRA Advantage	+$127,688	
Value of Account in 30 Years	$540,585	$244,692
Less Income Tax in Retirement (more realistically assuming lower tax bracket of 20%)	96,117	0
Net Amount	$444,468	$244,692
IRA Advantage	+$199,776	

will be taxed on $480,000. That tax comes to $168,000. After tax, the IRA investor in the 35 percent bracket would wind up with $372,000. *And that's $127,000 better than the individual who invested without an IRA.*

Now let's see what the figures look like if we assume, probably more realistically, that the IRA investor is only in the 20 percent bracket at retirement. You can reach the 20 percent range by being in the 15 percent bracket and adding some state or city taxes. At retirement, that bracket might frequently be lower, but I'm trying to be conservative, so let's call it 20 percent.

With $60,000 of his $540,000 ending money not taxable, the IRA investor will pay taxes on $480,000. At 20 percent the tax bite comes to $96,000. *That leaves the IRA holder with $444,000 at retirement, about $200,000 richer than the non-IRA investor, who only has $245,000 left.*

So you can see that, regardless of your tax bracket, you're much better off investing in an IRA even without the $2,000 tax-deductible contribution. Basically, that's because you don't suffer the leakages of taxes along the way. And those leakages turn into a torrent when you start compounding numbers after ten, twenty, or thirty years.

IRA TAX-DEFERRED BENEFITS

Another way to measure the benefits of an IRA is to see how much of your taxes are sheltered while your nest egg grows at compound interest. Table 7 shows the gains you can make if you deposit the maximum $2,000 tax-deferred a year, at 6 and 9 percent yields for your IRA.

At the end of a five-year period, if you earned only a 6 percent annual return, your account would be worth $11,951 and you would have deferred taxes on $1,951. If you continue to contribute $2,000 annually to your IRA over thirty years,

TABLE 7

TAX-DEFERRED IRA BENEFITS AT 6% AND 9% RETURNS
(Assuming $2,000 investment on the first of each year)

		AT 6% YIELD		AT 9% YIELD	
Years	Investment	IRA Value	Tax-Deferred Benefit	IRA Value	Tax-Deferred Benefit
1	2,000	2,120	120	2,180	180
5	10,000	11,951	1,951	13,047	3,047
10	20,000	27,943	7,943	33,121	13,121
20	40,000	77,985	37,985	111,529	71,529
30	60,000	167,603	107,603	297,151	237,151
40	80,000	328,095	248,095	736,584	656,000

your holdings would total $167,603 and you would have sheltered taxes on $107,603.

The figures naturally are more favorable at a 9 percent return. In five years your IRA would climb to $13,047 and you would have postponed paying taxes on $3,047. After thirty years at 9 percent, your IRA would be valued at $297,151 and you would have deferred taxes on $237,151.

Since the chances are that your tax rates at retirement will be lower than in your peak earning years, the tax-deferred benefits on an IRA take on even greater significance.

GAINS AT DIFFERENT TAX RATES

Let's examine the tax benefits of an IRA from another angle. Table 8 demonstrates how much you shelter at tax rates of 15, 28, and 35 percent. As you'll see, in five years, even at

TABLE 8

TAXES SHELTERED BY IRAs AT VARIOUS TAX BRACKETS
(Assuming $2,000 investment on the first of each year)

Years	15%	28%	35%
1	300	560	700
5	1,500	2,800	3,500
10	3,000	5,600	7,000
15	4,500	8,400	10,500
20	6,000	11,200	14,000
25	7,500	14,000	17,500
30	9,000	16,800	21,000
35	10,500	19,600	24,500
40	12,000	22,400	28,000

the lowly 15 percent level, you would have $1,500 more to work for you in your IRA. If your tax rate is 35 percent, you would have accumulated $3,500 more than if you had paid taxes on your IRA contribution each year.

If you look at the results after thirty years, you'll find that, even at the 15 percent rate, you would have deferred taxes of $9,000. At the 35 percent rate, you'd have $21,000 more at your disposal than if you had not invested in an IRA.

These figures, of course, would be doubled if you and your spouse both invest the maximum $2,000 each year. Thus, if you and your spouse are in the 28 percent bracket, you will shelter $33,600 in thirty years (that is, twice the $16,800 seen in Table 8 for the 28 percent column at thirty years).

The higher your tax bracket and the greater the return on your investment, the more you will benefit from your IRA. If you combine a high tax bracket—say, 35 percent—and earn a respectable 15 percent or so on your investment, the advantages of an IRA become irresistible.

CHAPTER 4

IRA—The Hype and the Highlights

If your bank IRAs were once the smart move, now it may be smarter for you to move elsewhere.
> —Oppenheimer Individual Retirement Account

* * * * *

How healthy is your IRA? We realize your potential.
> —Manufacturers Hanover Trust

* * * * *

You plan an active retirement. But have you told your IRA?
> —Franklin U.S. Government Securities Fund

* * * * *

T. Rowe Price puts real estate within reach . . . again. $5,000 minimum—$2,000 for IRAs.
> —T. Rowe Price Associates

* * * * *

The more you have in your IRA, the more options you should have for growth.
> —Marine Midland Bank

*   *   *   *   *

Locked in a bank IRA? Switch to the freedom of a Vanguard IRA.

—Vanguard Group

*   *   *   *   *

Start your Met Life IRA now. You'll feel better when the tax man cometh.

—Metropolitan Life

*   *   *   *   *

It's IRA season, and the buyer had better beware.

—Chilton Private Bank

*   *   *   *   *

Discover Magellan for your IRA.

—Fidelity Investments

*   *   *   *   *

Have you checked your IRA lately?

—The Dreyfus GNMA Fund

*   *   *   *   *

One bank offers the kind of IRAs that make everyone else's look tame.

—Citibank

*   *   *   *   *

Make your leap to IRA income. Call Boston.
                                        —The Boston Company

* * * * *

Make $25,000 from a $2,000 investment.
                                        —Chemical Bank

* * * * *

Are CDs your best option? Don't bank on it.
                                        —Scudder IRA Portfolio

* * * * *

Give your IRA more room to grow with an easy move to Schwab.
                                        —Charles Schwab

* * * * *

The Rushmore Fund IRA pays you 1% bonus instantly. It's anything but retiring.
                                        —The Rushmore Fund

* * * * *

If you're interested in retiring with $500,000, pick up the phone.
                                        —Allstate

* * * * *

Let's talk about retirement. Everybody's somebody at Dean Witter.

–Dean Witter Reynolds

*   *   *   *   *

Prescription for retirement.

–Medical Technology Fund

*   *   *   *   *

Shown above are only a few of the splashy ads pushing various IRA alternatives. During IRA season, there's no place to hide. It's impossible to read newspapers or magazines, listen to the radio, or watch television without being assaulted by a barrage of tempting advertisements designed to entice your hard-won dollars. No wonder. With IRAs, trustees can look forward to regular annual contributions (and early with-drawal penalties) which can continue to build for decades with young contributors.

That's why you're so popular and the bitterly fought-over centerpiece in a no-holds-barred economic tug-of-war of unprecedented proportions. And if you're confused by all the claims and promises and can't make up your mind where to place your retirement bets, let me try to give you a helping hand. I'd like to explore with you the most popular alterna-tives and provide solid, specific, tested advice on the best possible ways to invest your IRA. With my methods you will preserve your capital, enjoy complete liquidity, and protect yourself against inflation as well.

If you are reading this book, I assume you are one of the 40 million–plus wise Americans who already have an IRA and are interested in finding out how to make it grow as swiftly and as safely as possible. The likelihood is that you have had an IRA for several years and are already watching over a tidy sum.

When was the last time you totaled your accounts? If you haven't done it lately, I bet you'll be surprised at the size of your holdings. For example, if you have regularly put aside $2,000 each year since 1982, your accounts may now exceed $15,000. If your working spouse has been as conscientious as you, your combined IRAs may well be in the vicinity of $30,000. Now, that's a very respectable figure, and how you invest it deserves the most careful consideration. In subsequent chapters I'll make specific recommendations.

But first, on the chance that you have neglected to take advantage of this unique investment opportunity and are poised to take the plunge or are uncertain about any of the basic rules, here are a few things you ought to know.

WHAT IS AN IRA?

Simply put, an individual retirement account (IRA) is a savings plan that lets you set aside money for your retirement. Under the 1986 tax law, certain contributions are tax-deductible, while others are not. In either case, the earnings of your IRAs are not taxed until they are distributed to you.

The higher your tax bracket, the greater the advantage to you. Table 9 shows the equivalent return you need on a non-IRA investment to equal the yield on an IRA. For example, if you are in the 28 percent tax bracket, a 12 percent yield in a tax-sheltered IRA is equal to 16.7 percent on a non-IRA investment. If you are in the 35 percent bracket, that same 12 percent on an IRA is equal to an 18.5 percent return in a nonsheltered account.

TABLE 9

EQUIVALENT TAXABLE RETURNS AT VARIOUS IRA INVESTMENT YIELDS

% IRA Investment Yields	**TAX BRACKETS**		
	15%	28%	35%
5%	5.9%	6.9%	7.7%
6	7.1	8.3	9.2
7	8.2	9.7	10.8
8	9.4	11.1	12.3
9	10.6	12.5	13.8
10	11.8	13.9	15.4
11	12.9	15.3	16.9
12	14.1	16.7	18.5
13	15.3	18.1	20.0
14	16.5	19.4	21.5
15	17.7	20.8	23.1
16	18.8	22.2	24.6
17	20.0	23.6	26.2
18	21.2	25.0	27.7
19	22.4	26.4	29.2
20	23.5	27.8	30.8

WHO IS ELIGIBLE?

You are eligible to open an IRA if you are under seventy and a half years of age and receive compensation for personal services that must be included as taxable income for the year. The 1986 tax law has significantly revised the eligibility requirements for a tax-deductible IRA. Here, in simplified form, are the current rules:

• If neither you nor your spouse is covered by an employer-sponsored pension or profit-sharing plan, you are eligible for a tax-deductible IRA regardless of your income. Your status under the new law is unchanged from what it was previously.

• If you are a single individual with adjusted gross income under $25,000 or a couple with adjusted gross income under $40,000, your status is also unchanged from the previous rules. Regardless of any employer retirement plans, if you are single you can contribute $2,000 tax-deductible annually, and a working couple can contribute $4,000 tax-deductible.

• If covered by an employer pension or profit plan, single individuals with adjusted gross incomes between $25,000 and $35,000 and couples between $40,000 and $50,000 will see their tax-deductible contributions phased out proportionately as income rises. Thus, a single worker covered by a pension with an income of $30,000 can only enjoy a $1,000 tax-deductible contribution. For joint returns, working individuals can deduct $1,500 if adjusted gross income is $42,500; $1,000 if adjusted gross is $45,000; and $500 if adjusted gross is $47,500.

• Taxpayers subject to deductible limits can make additional nondeductible contributions. For example, a taxpayer with a $1,000 deductible IRA limit can also fund a $1,000 nondeductible IRA.

Naturally, the younger you are when you open an IRA, the more years you have to contribute and the greater the sum at your disposal when you retire. However, IRAs can be most advantageous even if you begin later in life. As you'll see in Table 10, if you start an IRA at age fifty, invest $2,000 annually at the start of each year, and earn 9 percent interest compounded, you'll have a total of $64,000 at age sixty-five and, if you don't retire until age seventy, your IRA will be worth $111,529. Table 11, assuming a 15 percent return, reveals that, with the same age fifty start-up, you would hold $99,961 at age sixty-five and $207,537 at age seventy.

TABLE 10

HOW YOUR IRA GROWS DEPENDING ON YOUR AGE WHEN YOU START
(Assuming $2,000 investment on the first of each year)

AT 9% INTEREST RATE

Your Present Age	IRA at Age 59	IRA at Age 65	IRA at Age 70
25	$429,422	$736,584	$1,146,733
30	270,615	470,250	736,584
35	167,402	297,151	470,250
40	100,320	184,648	297,151
45	56,722	111,529	184,648
50	28,386	64,007	111,529
55	9,969	33,121	64,007
60	–	13,047	33,047

QUALIFYING INCOME

Qualifying income for an IRA includes all compensation paid to you for work which you have performed. Compensation is generally defined as wages, salaries, tips, professional fees, bonuses, royalties, self-employment income, and other amounts you receive for providing personal services.

If you own and operate your own business as a sole proprietor, your net earnings, reduced by your deductible contributions to self-employment retirement plans, are considered compensation. If you are an active partner in a partnership, your share of partnership income, also reduced by deductible contributions to self-employment retirement plans, is compensation under IRA regulations.

TABLE 11

HOW YOUR IRA GROWS DEPENDING ON YOUR AGE WHEN YOU START
(Assuming $2,000 investment on the first of each year)

AT 15% INTEREST RATE

Your Present Age	IRA at Age 59	IRA at Age 65	IRA at Age 70
25	$1,385,140	$3,059,820	$5,906,493
30	711,573	1,581,350	3,059,820
35	361,742	813,474	1,581,350
40	180,050	414,665	813,474
45	85,685	207,537	414,665
50	36,675	99,961	207,537
55	11,220	44,089	99,961
60	–	15,071	15,071

All taxable alimony and separate maintenance payments received by an individual under a decree of divorce or separate maintenance are treated as compensation for tax years beginning after 1984.

INCOME NOT QUALIFYING UNDER IRA

Earnings on profits from property, such as rentals, and interest and dividend income are not considered compensation under IRA. If you invest in a partnership and do not provide service, your share of partnership income is not compensation. The term "compensation" also does not include any amounts received as a pension or annuity, or as deferred compensation. Retirement income is not considered compensation for purposes of making deductible contributions to an IRA.

AMOUNT OF CONTRIBUTIONS

Under present regulations, each year you can contribute up to $2,000 or the amount of your earned compensation, whichever is less. In other words, if you earn only $1,500 in covered compensation, that entire amount can go into your IRA. You are permitted to combine income from various sources. For example, if you earn $1,000 from part-time employment in an office and another $1,000 as an actor or a writer, you would be eligible to make the maximum $2,000 contribution for the year. The tax-deductibility of your contribution is dependent on the criteria described earlier in this chapter.

If you have no compensation in any year or wish to skip a year for any reason, that's okay—but you cannot make up the omitted amount in any subsequent year. Nevertheless, you can keep in your IRA the amounts you contributed in previous years. You can resume making and deducting contributions for any subsequent years for which you are eligible.

What if you and your spouse both earn compensation? Well, the same rules apply, making $4,000 the top annual contribution for a husband and wife. Should your spouse have insufficient compensation in any year, you can contribute an additional $250 to a separate "spousal" IRA for a combined total of $2,250. As you'll see in Table 12, a "spousal" IRA makes a lot of sense. At a 9 percent return, $2,250 contributed annually would grow to $334,295 in thirty years, and at 17 percent, it would climb to $1,704,386!

You may split your contributions to the two IRAs any way you wish as long as you do not contribute more than $2,000 to either IRA for any year. In addition, you cannot roll over assets from your account to your spouse's account. Joint accounts are not permitted for IRAs but, with a spousal IRA, you must file a joint tax return.

There is no rule that says you must make your IRA

TABLE 12

GROWTH OF SPOUSAL IRA
(Assuming $2,250 investment on the first of each year)

Years	6%	9%	12%	15%	17%
5	$ 13,445	$ 14,678	$ 16,009	$ 17,446	$ 18,466
10	31,436	37,261	44,223	52,536	58,950
15	55,513	72,008	93,945	123,114	147,710
20	87,733	125,470	181,572	265,073	342,312
25	130,852	207,729	336,002	550,602	768,966
30	188,553	334,295	608,158	1,124,902	1,704,386
35	265,771	529,031	1,087,793	2,280,026	3,755,239
40	369,107	828,657	1,933,076	4,602,263	8,251,616

contribution in one lump sum. You may make as many contributions to total $2,000 that your financial institution permits. If you fund your IRA through weekly or monthly payroll deductions, that's fine, too. You can also make your IRA contribution by withdrawing savings or cashing any of your other assets. The only requirement is that you must earn compensation for personal services equivalent to the amount you place in your IRA. All contributions must be in cash, check, or money order. You cannot deduct contributions of property.

CONTRIBUTION DEADLINES

Your IRA contributions for any year must be made by April 15 of the following year. For example, you can make your 1987 contribution from January 1, 1987, through April 15, 1988.

Under certain circumstances, you can contribute $4,000

in the first quarter of any year. Let's say you have not made your 1987 contribution. You can contribute for both 1987 and 1988 between January 1 and April 15, 1988. For any contribution you make in the first quarter of any year just be sure that your financial institution credits your account for the proper year to which your contribution should be applied.

While your IRA contributions are acceptable up to the tax filing deadline, it would be to your advantage to put your money in as early each year as is possible. The sooner you make the contributions, the longer they will be earning tax-deferred interest, dividends, or capital gains. Specifically, if you make your contribution at the start of the year on January 1, it will accumulate tax-deferred interest between that date and the April 15 deadline of the following year—an additional fifteen and a half months of earnings. And the difference can be substantial. For example, if you made your contributions at the earliest possible date rather than the latest, your earnings at a 10 percent return would be enhanced by $3,979 after ten years, $14,440 after twenty years, and $41,570 after thirty years. That's right. Your "start-of-the-year" IRA would be worth $361,887 after thirty years compared with the "tax deadline" IRA of $318,317.

Suppose you're not that great a procrastinator and wait to make your $2,000 IRA investment on December 31 rather than January 1 of each year. As you'll see in Tables 13 and 14, it will also cost you a bundle. If you earn a 10 percent return and invest on January 1 of each year, you'll have $361,887 at the end of thirty years compared with $328,988 if you wait until December 31, a difference of $32,899. At a 17 percent return, the difference in your IRA after thirty years would be $220,130! So the early bird gets more than the worm.

If you file your tax return for any year before the deadline—say, in January—you can deduct your IRA contribution on your return before you actually make it, so long

TABLE 13

SAVINGS BY EARLY IRA DEPOSITS
($2,000 contributions each year, compounded annually)

AT 10% RETURN

End of Year	INVESTMENTS ON		
	Jan. 1	Dec. 31	Difference
1	$ 2,200	$ 2,000	+ $ 200
5	13,431	12,210	+ 1,221
10	35,062	31,875	+ 3,187
15	69,900	63,545	+ 6,355
20	126,005	114,550	+ 11,455
25	216,364	196,694	+ 19,670
30	361,887	328,988	+ 37,899
35	596,254	542,049	+ 54,205
40	973,704	885,186	+ 88,518

as it is put in before April 15. *You cannot advance this IRA due date with any tax filing extensions.* Should your income tax refund arrive in time, you can even use it to make that year's IRA contribution.

You may benefit from an IRA contribution even if you don't itemize the deductions on your tax return. Simply list your IRA total contribution as "adjustments to income" on your 1040 form.

Warning: There is a penalty if you contribute over your permitted amount in a single year. Not only may you not deduct the excess when calculating your income tax, you must also pay a 6 percent excise tax on the extra money each year it stays in the account.

TABLE 14

SAVINGS BY EARLY IRA DEPOSITS
($2,000 contributions each year, compounded annually)

AT 17% RETURN

End of Year	INVESTMENTS ON		
	Jan. 1	Dec. 31	Difference
1	$ 2,340	$ 2,000	+$ 340
5	16,414	14,029	+ 2,385
10	52,400	44,786	+ 7,614
15	131,298	112,220	+ 19,078
20	304,277	260,066	+ 44,211
25	683,525	584,209	+ 99,316
30	1,515,010	1,294,880	+ 220,130
35	3,337,990	2,852,980	+ 485,010
40	7,334,770	6,269,040	+ 1,065,730

AGE REQUIREMENTS

The only age requirement for contribution to an IRA is that you must be under seventy and a half. You must begin withdrawals from your IRA by April 1 following the year you reach seventy and a half. At that time you can either withdraw the entire amount and pay tax on that sum, purchase an insurance annuity with your IRA, or take out minimum annual amounts over a permissible period based on your life expectancy or the joint life expectancy of yourself and a designated beneficiary. *Note:* The IRS is considering "unisex" life expectancy tables that have not been approved at this writing.

At age seventy and a half, the life expectancy of a male owner of an IRA is currently considered to be 12.1 years while

TABLE 15

INDIVIDUAL IRS LIFE EXPECTANCY MULTIPLES

LIFE EXPECTANCY (NO. OF YEARS)

Present Age	Males	Females
70	12.1	15.0
71	11.6	14.4
72	11.0	13.8
73	10.5	13.2
74	10.1	12.6
75	9.6	12.1
76	9.1	11.6
77	8.7	11.0
78	8.3	10.5
79	7.8	10.1
80	7.5	9.6
81	7.1	9.1
82	6.7	8.7
83	6.3	8.3
84	6.0	7.8
85	5.7	7.5
86	5.4	7.1
87	5.1	6.7
88	4.8	6.3
89	4.5	6.0
90	4.2	6.0

that of a female IRA owner is 15 years. Table 15 shows the actuarial figures for minimum required distributions for individuals under current IRS rules.

As you'll note from Table 15, a seventy-and-a-half-year-old man must take out at least one twelfth (1/12.1) of his IRA holdings in the first year while a woman must withdraw at least one fifteenth (1/15). In the following year, the man must take out at least one eleventh (1/11.6) and the female one fourteenth (1/14.4) of the remainder. The accounts continue to appreciate after you begin withdrawals. If your investments are wise enough, the growth of your account can replenish the withdrawals.

If you would like to keep your distributions at a minimum, the IRS permits you to calculate a joint multiple with your spouse. Table 16 shows the joint life expectancy of an individual at age seventy and a half and his or her spouse.

Here's how you make your calculation of minimum permissible distributions from Table 16. Suppose a male is aged seventy and a half and his spouse is sixty-seven. If you look at the age sixty-seven column, you'll see that the male multiple is 19.7 years for joint life expectancy. If the female is seventy and a half and the male beneficiary sixty-seven, the joint life expectancy is 19.2 years.

For the purposes of this example, let's assume that the IRA stands at $100,000. If the joint life expectancy is 19.7 years, the minimum permissible annual distribution is $100,000 divided by 19.7, or $5,076. If the joint life expectancy is 19.2 years, the minimum annual distribution would be $5,208.

Be sure to calculate your minimum annual take-outs very carefully because there's a stiff IRS penalty of 50 percent on any excess accumulation not withdrawn in any year. For instance, suppose you were required to withdraw a minimum of $5,000 each year and took out only $4,000, a difference of $1,000. You would have to pay a penalty tax of half that sum, or $500.

When you approach seventy and a half, I suggest that you consult your IRA trustee and your accountant to determine what is best for your individual circumstance at that time.

Should you wish, you can start withdrawing IRA money without penalty when you reach age fifty-nine and a half, with all withdrawals taxed as ordinary income in the year received. If you are earning qualifying income, you may continue

TABLE 16

Age of Spouse in Year IRA Owner Becomes 70½	JOINT LIFE EXPECTANCY (NUMBER OF YEARS)	
	Female-Multiple IRA Owner	Male-Multiple IRA Owner
61	21.6	23.0
62	21.1	22.4
63	20.7	21.8
64	20.3	21.2
65	19.9	20.7
66	19.6	20.2
67	19.2	19.7
68	18.9	19.2
69	18.6	18.7
70	18.3	18.3
71	18.0	17.9
72	17.8	17.5
73	17.5	17.1
74	17.3	16.7
75	17.1	16.4
76	16.9	16.1
77	16.7	15.8
78	16.6	15.5
79	16.4	15.2
80	16.3	14.9
81	16.2	14.7
82	16.0	14.5
83	15.9	14.3
84	15.8	14.1
85	15.8	13.9
86	15.7	13.7
87	15.6	13.6
88	15.5	13.4
89	15.5	13.3
90	15.4	13.2

contributing to an IRA until the year in which you reach seventy and a half, even though you are also making withdrawals from it.

The 1986 tax law requires individuals to combine their deductible and nondeductible IRAs and pay tax on a prorated portion considered withdrawn from the deductible IRA and earnings in either type of IRA.

As an example, let's assume a taxpayer has $10,000 in IRAs—$8,000 in a deductible account and $2,000 in a new nondeductible account without earnings. If he withdraws $1,000, only 20 percent—or $200—would be considered coming from the nondeductible IRA on which he has already paid taxes. The remaining $800 would be from the deductible IRA and be taxed at his regular rate.

If you withdraw money from your IRA before you reach age fifty-nine and a half, you'll have to pay a 10 percent penalty on the amount withdrawn as well as your regular tax. That penalty is waived if money is withdrawn in equal installments over a lifetime, such as through an annuity.

There is no withdrawal penalty under age fifty-nine and a half if you are permanently disabled. The IRS rules on "disabled" are very tough. If a condition can be corrected, it is not a disability. To be considered disabled, you must be "unable to engage in any substantial gainful activity" and have a condition which is expected to last a long time or to lead to death. Should you die, your beneficiary can withdraw the money in your account without tax penalty.

INVESTMENT AREAS

There is no rule that you must restrict your IRA to a single trustee or custodian, but it must be established in the United States. You can make your contributions to banks and other savings institutions, mutual funds, brokerage houses, insurance companies, and any other qualifying trustee.

Several investment areas are ineligible for IRA funding. These include life insurance policies (annuities are okay); and, since 1982, acquiring anything under the category of "collectibles," which includes metals, gems, works of art, antiques, rugs, coins (except gold or silver coins issued by the U.S. Government), stamps, alcoholic beverages, and certain other tangible property. However, you can participate indirectly in certain proscribed areas by investing in gold and silver stocks or mutual funds and in commodities and real estate with specialized investment funds.

You can set up as many IRAs as you wish as long as your combined annual contributions to all of them do not exceed $2,000, or $2,250 for a spousal IRA. Each IRA can have a separate beneficiary.

More detailed information on IRAs will be found in IRS Publication 590, "Individual Retirement Arrangements," updated annually and available free from the Internal Revenue Service.

KEOGH PLANS

No discussion of retirement programs would be complete without a reference to Keogh plans, another option provided by the IRS. Only persons with self-employment earnings can set up or contribute to a Keogh plan. These earnings must originate from a business in which your services materially helped to produce income. Virtually every business or profession qualifies under this category. You can have income from property that your personal efforts helped create, such as books or inventions on which you earn royalties. Earned income includes net earnings from selling or otherwise disposing of property, but it does not include capital gains or interest income.

Keogh plans are much more complicated and have much higher contribution limits than do IRAs. There are several types of Keogh plans including profit-sharing, money-purchase, and defined benefit, with different rules covering them.

If your income comes from self-employment, you may be eligible for both an IRA and a Keogh plan. If you are covered by a Keogh plan, your ability to make a deductible IRA contribution depends upon your adjusted gross income level.

There are different deadlines for opening Keogh and IRA plans. You must open a Keogh plan by the end of the year for which you are making contributions, although you can postpone your final contribution until your tax filing date. Unlike the rule for IRAs, the deadline for making the final contribution to Keogh plans is carried forward to the date of any extension you receive.

While there are similarities between Keogh plans and IRAs, there are many differences. If you have a tax adviser, it would be wise to consult him as to your rights and responsibilities under Keogh plans. You might also want to consult IRS Publication 560, "Self-employed Retirement Plans," available free from the Internal Revenue Service.

MAKING CHANGES

You can personally withdraw any IRA account and move it yourself (called a rollover) to another trustee once a year without penalty as long as you reinvest the entire amount within sixty days. *A note of caution:* If you fail to reinvest the IRA funds within sixty days, the money is considered cashed in and you must report it as ordinary income—plus paying a 10 percent penalty if you're under age fifty-nine and a half.

Under certain circumstances, rollovers into an IRA or IRAs can be made from a qualified employer pension plan. This is usually a lump-sum distribution after a job change. Once the shift is made, the accounts involved are subject to the same IRA rollover and transfer rules as any other IRA.

If you never take personal possession of the assets, you can arrange as many trustee-to-trustee shifts (called direct transfers) as you wish. Generally, if you move your money within a single family of funds, you can arrange the shift with just a phone call. The direct transfer method is the one I prefer and use. It's an integral part of my IRA investment technique that will be explored fully in subsequent chapters.

CHAPTER 5

IRA Investment Options—
An Overview

One of the most important financial decisions you will ever make is your choice of an IRA investment vehicle. Here are a few vital facts to consider:

1. *The number of years to retirement . . . and your goals.* Your stage in life is paramount in deciding how to structure your IRA program. If you are, say, thirty-five to forty years old and well launched on a career, you probably would be interested primarily in accumulating capital. Based on the relative risks you are willing to accept, your best bet would be investments linked to the stock market. Stocks surpass other investments in the long run, as we will demonstrate later. However, if you are sixty-two years old with only three years to go before retirement, there is little point in going into stocks because you don't have the time for the investment to work for you. For older people, I would advocate money market funds or certificates of deposit (CDs).

2. *The amount of risk you feel comfortable with.* How much risk you want to tolerate is a purely personal decision related to but not necessarily dependent upon your age. Temperament is an important factor. Some people just enjoy the excitement of gambling on the prospect of a significantly higher return while others prefer the peace of mind of a lower-yielding but completely guaranteed investment. It's your choice and, as you'll see, there are various appropriate alternatives

regardless of how aggressive or conservative your investment philosophy may be. Whatever you decide, be sure you won't lie awake at night worrying about your decision.

3. *What fees are involved—custodian trustee fees, transaction costs, and other charges.* The factor of fees is something everyone must realistically consider. Specifics are spelled out in every prospectus and should be carefully studied. What you are interested in is the bottom line—your net proceeds after all charges.

4. *Whether you retain the flexibility to change your investment program if conditions warrant.* Economic conditions such as inflation and interest rates and the direction of the stock market can change rapidly. Therefore, it would be to your advantage to be able to adjust your investment strategy quickly and easily. The investment procedure which I will detail later provides just such an alternative.

In the following pages I will briefly highlight the most popular IRA investment options, reserving in-depth consideration of CDs, stocks, and bonds for the three following chapters.

BANKS

Here you can select commercial banks, savings banks, savings and loan associations, and credit unions, all of which have similar features. Most bank-type IRA investments are in savings accounts and in certificates of deposit (CDs). Let's examine the perceived advantages of bank accounts.

Savings Accounts

1. *You can withdraw your money at any time.* But remember, if IRA money is involved, you'll have to pay a substantial 10 percent penalty if your withdrawal is made before you reach fifty-nine and a half or are disabled.

2. *You have the security of knowing exactly what your retirement nest egg will be.* That's partly true. However, bank interest rates do change and the rate of return on traditional savings accounts is generally a good deal less than you can earn in other equally safe investments. At this writing, many banks are still paying as low as 5½ percent on their savings accounts.

3. *Your money is insured by state or federal agencies.* Well, in recent years we've seen some problems where state agencies are involved. Insurance by the Federal Deposit Insurance Corporation (FDIC) or the Federal Savings and Loan Insurance Corporation (FSLIC) is limited to $100,000 per IRA deposit in an insured bank. (If you have other deposits in an insured bank, they are insured up to an additional $100,000.) Now, $100,000 may seem like a lot of money, but that's a sum within reach in most IRAs. So, in time, you would have to shop around for additional banks.

Certificates of Deposit (CDs or Time Deposits)

The main difference between a CD and a traditional savings account is that the CD must be on deposit for a specified time. Generally, the longer the term of deposit, the higher the interest rate. If you withdraw money prior to the maturity date of the CD, you will usually have to pay a penalty equivalent to three or six months' interest on the amount withdrawn.

If you select a CD, you can choose either a fixed or a variable rate of interest over a fixed term. The variable rates are frequently linked to short-term investments such as 26-week Treasury bills and are adjusted on either a weekly or a monthly basis. Fixed rates would be advantageous if interest rates are declining, and variable rates would be more beneficial if rates are rising. In either case, you are locked in with your choice for the term of deposit and face a substantial penalty if you want to move your money.

It's important to be alert about when your specified term of investment ends. If you make no new choice when the bank notifies you of term expiration, your CD will be renewed or "rolled over" under the then existing rates for a similar term.

A note on interest rates, tax-exempts, and capital gains under IRA regulations: Although the interest earned on bank accounts is fully taxable, that's not a consideration for IRAs because these earnings accumulate tax-deferred. Actually, for IRA purposes, there's no advantage in buying tax-exempt bonds because all IRA earnings are tax-deferred until you withdraw funds. Under the 1986 law, all capital gains are taxed at ordinary income rates.

Money Market Deposit Accounts
Banks and savings and loan associations offer money market deposit accounts (MMDAs) based on high-quality, short-term debt obligations issued by the U.S. Government and large corporations. MMDAs are federally insured up to $100,000 in covered institutions.

MUTUAL FUNDS

A mutual fund is a company supervised by professional managers whose sole business is investing in a portfolio of securities, usually stocks, bonds, and money market instruments, or a combination of these. It sells shares to investors, whose subsequent returns come from distributed dividends earned by the fund's assets and proceeds from profitable market transactions. Of course there is no guarantee of profit. The net assets of the fund fluctuate on the basis of the fund's performance. Shares can be redeemed at any time.

Most mutual funds are known as "open-end" investment companies. That's because they stand ready to sell new shares to you at any time and will buy them back whenever you wish at the then current asset value of the shares. Since funds create new shares as new money is invested, the number of shares is unlimited, or open-ended. Closed-end funds issue only a fixed number of shares that generally are bought and sold on the stock market. These shares usually sell at a premium over the net asset value or at a discount below it.

Federally regulated, mutual funds are mandated to pay out at least 90 percent of their net income to shareholders each year. In addition to providing a single certificate representing your ownership in a portion of a large number of equities, mutual funds offer extreme liquidity. It's very easy to buy and sell their shares.

Mutual funds have two basic structures: *no-load funds*, which are usually sold through the mail and have no sales fees, and *load funds*, which are offered by brokerage houses and financial institutions at sales commissions. When you purchase a load fund, you pay the net asset value plus the sales charge. For example, if you buy into a load fund which charges a 9.3 percent commission and invest $1,000, your holdings will be worth only $907, with the remainder going for a sales fee.

Table 17 shows the difference in the growth of your IRA if your investments are made with a 9.3 percent commission paid to a load fund and with a no-load fund. Assuming $2,000 invested annually at a constant 15 percent rate of return, your IRA would total $215,593 at the end of twenty years at a 9.3 percent commission and $235,620 if there were no load, a difference of $20,027. At the end of forty years, the IRA with commission would come to $3,744,103 against $4,091,900 no-load, a difference of $347,797.

Important: The caliber of a fund's performance bears no relationship to the presence or absence of a sales charge. Because of the savings involved, I buy only no-load funds and I strongly recommend that you do likewise.

For the investor, mutual funds provide many advantages. First, the fund has a large pool of capital which permits

TABLE 17

DIFFERENCE IN IRA INVESTMENT GROWTH
WITH LOAD AND NO-LOAD FUNDS
(Assuming $2,000 investment on the first of each year
with 15% annual yield)

Year	IRA with 9.3% Commission	IRA with No Load	Difference
1	$ 2,105	$ 2,300	$ 195
5	14,189	15,508	1,319
10	42,729	46,699	3,970
15	100,133	109,435	9,302
20	215,593	235,620	20,027
25	447,824	489,424	41,600
30	914,923	999,913	84,990
35	1,854,427	2,026,690	172,263
40	3,744,103	4,091,900	347,797

assets to be bought and sold at significantly lower transaction costs. Second, the mutual fund offers the investor far greater diversification than he can acquire on his own. Each share in a mutual fund is based on a broad range of securities, thus reducing the risk should any one company or industry group fall on hard times. Finally, mutual funds are run by professional managers who are gauged by their results. They devote themselves full-time to research and analysis of various investment options—and the records of their performance are readily available.

According to final 1985 IRA estimates by the Investment Company Institute, mutual funds had 7.9 million IRA accounts valued at $31.6 billion at the end of 1985, giving the industry a 15.8 percent market share—up from 12.5 percent a year earlier. Assets of mutual funds almost doubled, increasing 92 percent, while assets of depository institutions (commercial banks, mutual savings and loan associations) increased by 34 percent.

Table 18 shows the estimated value of all IRA plans in billions of dollars, together with the percent of market share held by the various institutions.

You can find a mutual fund to cater to virtually every investment objective. Broadly speaking, the various funds can be divided into income funds, growth funds, growth and income funds, aggressive growth funds, balanced funds, corporate bond funds, government income funds, GNMA funds, option/income funds, special-interest funds, and money market funds. A breakdown of mutual fund IRAs by investment objective will be found in Table 19.

The classifications of mutual funds are almost self-explanatory but let's run through them in case there's some confusion.

Income Funds

Tending to be among the most conservative funds, these have as their primary goal high current income. Investments are in large, well-established companies with little price volatility. Many of the holdings pay regular substantial dividends. Capital gains are a secondary consideration. Half of their assets are usually in income-producing stocks, with the remainder in convertibles and straight debt instruments.

Growth Funds

Here the aim is capital appreciation. Most investments are in securities that are expected to grow in value over a long period of time. Generally, these holdings include large-capitalization stocks like International Business Machines, General Motors, and General Electric. These funds will benefit in bull markets although not as much as maximum capital

TABLE 18

ESTIMATED VALUE OF IRA PLANS
(In billions of dollars and percent market share)

	12/81		12/82		12/83		12/84		12/85	
Commercial Banks	$ 5.8	22.5%	$13.6	25.9%	$26.5	29.0%	$ 37.2	28.2%	$ 51.5	25.8%
Mutual Savings Banks	3.4	13.1	4.7	8.9	6.5	7.1	9.3	7.0	11.9	6.0
Savings & Loans	10.7	41.0	15.6	29.8	25.2	27.6	34.1	25.8	44.5	22.3
Life Insurance Companies	3.3	12.7	5.8	11.1	9.0	9.9	12.6	9.5	16.9	8.5
Credit Unions	0.2	0.8	1.6	3.0	5.0	5.5	7.8	5.9	13.9	6.9
Mutual Funds	2.6	9.9	5.7	10.8	10.7	11.7	16.5	12.5	31.6	15.8
Self-directed	N/A		5.5	10.5	8.4	9.2	14.6	11.1	29.4	14.7
Total IRA Dollar Value	$26.1		$52.4		$91.3		$132.1		$199.8	

Source: Investment Company Institute, 1600 M Street, Washington, D.C. 20036.

gains funds. However they will not decline as much in bear markets. They are more stable, less volatile, and perform more consistently than the more aggressive growth funds.

Growth and Income Funds

These seek investments in stable companies which are expected to pay high dividends and have the potential for capital growth. As a result, they generally pay the biggest dividends in the growth-fund category. The performance of these funds generally broadly reflects the performance of the market as a whole.

Aggressive Growth Funds

Also known as "maximum capital gains" and "performance" funds, these are the riskier high rollers who aim for

TABLE 19

MUTUAL FUNDS IRAs
BY INVESTMENT OBJECTIVE

Investment Objective	% Assets as of 12/31/85
Aggressive Growth	11.9%
Growth	13.7
Growth & Income	12.8
Precious Metals	0.8
International	5.9
Balanced	0.6
Income	2.0
Government Income	10.8
GNMA	7.0
Corporate Bond	11.4
Option/Income	2.6
Money Market	20.5

Source: Investment Company Institute.

big capital gains by investing in start-up or small and, they hope, rapidly growing companies and in companies and industries which are suffering difficult times and are temporarily out of favor. They also may engage in borrowing money to provide leverage, short selling, hedging, options, and warrants. In addition to using specialized investment techniques, they may also do short-term trading. These funds frequently outperform broad averages in bull markets and drop further during bear markets.

Balanced Funds

As the name implies, these funds usually carry fixed ratios of common and preferred stocks, money market instruments, and bonds to protect against roller-coaster market conditions. Their objectives are to preserve principal, pay current income, and achieve long-term growth of both principal and income. Because of their defensive nature vis-à-vis capital preservation, they are relatively low-risk investments.

Corporate Bond Funds

The amount of risk depends on the particular fund's objectives. The holdings can range from low-grade, high-yielding so-called junk bonds to blue chips and may include zero coupon bonds. Maturities on zero coupon bonds range up to thirty years. These bonds sell at deep discounts until redeemed at full face value. Zero coupon bonds are issued by the Treasury, large corporations, and tax-exempt institutions.

Government Income Funds

Of primary interest to people in high tax brackets who are seeking tax-free income, these funds are of relatively little benefit to IRA and Keogh investors. If you want to invest in bonds, you are better served by higher-yielding securities whose interest compounds on a tax-deferred basis.

GNMA or Ginnie Mae Funds

To qualify for this category, the majority of the fund's portfolio must always be invested in mortgage securities backed by the Government National Mortgage Association.

Option/Income Funds

These funds aim for a high current return by investing primarily in dividend-paying common stocks on which call options are traded on national securities exchanges. Income generally consists of dividends, premiums from writing call options, net short-term gains from sales of portfolio securities on exercises of options, and any profits from closing purchase transactions.

Special Interest Funds

These are funds that concentrate on specific industries or areas—gold and precious metals, energy, foreign holdings, medical stocks, social investments, and other limited sectors.

Money Market Funds

Money market funds run by mutual funds are a popular IRA investment vehicle. A typical portfolio might include various U.S. Government agency and Treasury obligations (often guaranteed as to principal and interest), large-denomination bank certificates of deposit (far above the $100,000 per depositor insurance provided by federal agencies), corporate obligations such as bonds and promissory notes, letters of credit drawn on banks, and bankers' acceptances used to finance various projects. You may also find so-called repurchase agreement (repos) or U.S. Treasury certificates which the fund buys and resells to the seller at a later, agreed-upon date, and Eurodollar CDs (deposits by a U.S. branch in overseas branches). While money market funds are not federally insured, they are liquid and extremely safe. These funds play a major role in my basic investment strategy and you'll read more about them in subsequent chapters.

REITs

Another area of special-interest investing involves real estate investment trusts (REIT). These are public companies that acquire investment properties and issue mortgages. Shares in REITs, which are bought and sold through brokers, register gains when rental income is high and properties are sold at a profit. The law requires that REITs pay out 95 percent of their rental or mortgage income as dividends to shareholders.

ANNUITIES

An annuity is the most common IRA provided by insurance companies. The company invests your IRA contribution, and the size of your annuity depends on the amount of your contributions and the investment earnings. The ultimate payout to you may be at a predetermined fixed rate or at a variable rate based on the performance of the investment fund.

SELF-DIRECTED IRAs

Should you wish, you can even set up a "self-directed" IRA with many brokers. This will permit you to trade stocks and bonds the same way as you would without an IRA. Of course, you will pay your broker the usual transaction charges and probably an annual fee as well.

*   *   *   *   *

Although you can trade stocks and bonds on your own under IRA, I think you'll do a lot better with the right mutual funds. You'll recall that an important feature of investing in a family of mutual funds is that you can transfer your IRA from one fund to another quickly and without cost. This gives you great flexibility to adjust to changing economic and market conditions.

The IRA approach that I use for many investors who have entrusted their funds to my management involves switching between no-load common stock funds and money market funds, depending on the current momentum of the stock market. My IRA strategy is consistent with my overall philosophy: Be fully invested in stocks when the indicators are positive—such as when interest rates are falling—and move into cash when indicators are negative—such as when the Federal Reserve raises bank reserve requirements. This IRA investment technique has proven extremely profitable. In subsequent chapters, I'll explain exactly how you can manage your investment in the same way. The trick is in the timing. The procedure is not very complicated and yields most rewarding results.

CHAPTER 6

Baseball and Stocks— Which Ball Park Are You Playing In?

*A*s we explore in depth the wide range of investment options available, I will present vital statistics on the historic rates of return for the various alternatives discussed. In considering these figures, it is important to understand their context.

Different monetary and economic conditions prevailed during many of these years, and these shaped the figures we will be reviewing. Returns that seemed "high" at certain times were really "low" when adjusted for inflation.

Although all investments are affected by the economic climate, I would like to discuss briefly how stock performances can be distorted by differences in the economic environment. To help clarify my comments, I'll offer a baseball analogy.

Aside from the stock market, baseball has been my greatest interest ever since I was a youngster. I've always loved to pore over baseball statistics and analyze the game. In some ways, what I do for the stock market nowadays is not very different from what I used to do for baseball. Both endeavors require examining a lot of numerical data and trying to make sense out of it. Interestingly, some of the yardsticks which I found useful in baseball also apply to stocks. I'll show you some examples.

The other night I was flipping the channels on my television set and stopped long enough to watch a college baseball game between Michigan and Minnesota for a few minutes. They were playing in the new domed stadium in Minneapolis on artificial turf with aluminum bats. A shadow was cast across the pitcher's mound from what must have been a piece of the ceiling or the upper deck. It drew a black line from third base, across the mound, over to first base. I sat there watching this for a couple of minutes trying to figure out what the funny black line was.

Then I heard the plink of the bat several times. Not that great sounding crack that I love on opening day in a big league ball park. No. It was a definite plink. A sound almost as obnoxious as when you run your fingernail down a blackboard. I began to wonder what this thing was I was watching. It couldn't have been baseball. Domes, weird shadows, artificial turf, and aluminum bats. It wasn't the game I used to know.

Well, you might like this new version of baseball, you might not. That's not the point. What struck me is the effect these elements have on the game. The ball carries a lot further when struck with an aluminum bat. That means more base hits and far more home runs. The artificial turf also tends to carry the ball faster on a bounce than it would on regular grass. And who knows what effect the dome itself might have?

Now suppose all games in a major league season were played in that dome using those atrocious aluminum bats. Batting averages and home runs would be inflated versus games played on conventional grass in an outdoor ball park. If someone hit forty home runs and batted .300 under such conditions, would he really be a good hitter or just a medium hitter who had a fairly decent year? Or possibly, would he be mediocre? It's hard to say.

One thing is for sure: You'd have to study the long-run effects of these factors on the game and then make adjustments to batting averages, earned run averages, and the like if you wanted to compare performances played with metal bats versus wood bats, artificial turf versus grass, and so forth.

Let's try a different tack. I recently read the *Bill James Baseball Abstract 1986*, and, as always, I'll immerse myself in those statistics for another year. James's work often flies in the face of conventional wisdom. He attempts an unbiased scientific approach to analyzing the game, then backs it up with empirical testing. That's the same method I've employed with the stock market over the fifteen years that I've been writing *The Zweig Forecast*. Let me try to relate baseball to stocks.

According to James, what American League team has the lowest earned run average in road games in the past decade? I doubt that 1 percent of fans would get the answer: the Boston Red Sox. After all, everyone "knows" the Red Sox always have lousy pitching and good hitting. In truth, it only seems that way.

The problem is that the Red Sox play in Fenway Park, a weird antiquated stadium that's a paradise for hitters and a nightmare for pitchers. Runs—lots of them—are scored in Fenway relative to any other American League park. Since the Sox play half their games there, their earned run averages look crummy and their batting averages seem terrific.

But if you examine only their road games, played in thirteen other parks, you get a more accurate reflection of their pitching and hitting, since their "ball park effect" of high run scoring is eliminated. The opposite effect—very few runs—occurs in Houston's Astrodome. It always appears that the Astros' hitters are weak and their pitchers strong.

A similar problem confronts us in the stock market—namely, in which park are we playing at any given moment? High-run (bullish) Fenway or the low-run (bearish) Astrodome? Suppose batting averages and earned run averages are analogous to technical and fundamental indicators. Is a dividend yield on the Dow of, say, 4 percent bullish or bearish?

Is a price/earnings ratio of 15 on the Standard & Poor's 500 Index too high or too low? Well, there are no meaningful answers to such questions unless you know where the stock market ball game is being played.

If inflation were low and dying, the Federal Reserve easing, interest rates dropping, and government generally pro-business, it's akin to playing in Fenway Park with the wind blowing out . . . tons of runs will be scored (or money made in a bull market). Conversely, rapid inflation, a tight Fed, higher rates, and a nasty government would shift the game to the Astrodome . . . lots of shutouts (and bear market losses).

So it's crucial to examine the major monetary and economic background for stocks before analyzing to death the popular technical and fundamental indicators. What's "overbought," "too optimistic," or "too pricey" in the Astrodome might be just fine in Fenway. Moreover, most of the stock market games from 1966 to mid-1982 were played in the hostile environment (for runs or for bulls) of the Astrodome. For the bulk of time since then (as this is written in mid-1986), the game has moved to Fenway . . . but most observers are still looking at the batting averages of 1966–82 as benchmarks. It won't work.

Suppose in all ball parks an average of four runs are scored a game per team. If a club were up to five runs a game, you might think they have great hitters; down to three a game, you'd suppose they stink. But five runs a game might well be normal for Fenway while three a game could be the Astrodome average.

As I write this, everyone's counting five runs in the stock market and saying, "That's too many runs . . . it can't be sustained . . . no team can keep scoring that much . . . especially since up until four years ago teams were only scoring three runs a game." My point is that five runs is merely "average" if the game is in Fenway . . . and perhaps we shouldn't worry until we're seeing six or seven runs a game . . . or more important, not to worry until the game shifts to a less bullish ball park (which it could).

IMPACT OF INFLATION ON IRAs

The monetary "ball park" in which you play out your retirement years holds the key to whether your IRA makes you a winner or a loser. For it is the prevailing rate of inflation in the years ahead that will determine what your IRA will ultimately be worth in purchasing power.

As an example, suppose you are gearing your IRA investments to score a modest $1,000 a month after you retire. Let's see what varying rates of inflation will do to your game plan.

Please take a look at Table 20, which shows the effects of different rates of inflation on a planned $1,000 a month

TABLE 20

EFFECTS OF INFLATION ON VALUE OF IRA PAYOUTS

(What $1,000 monthly in today's dollars would be worth at various inflation rates over 40 years)

Years	3%	5%	7%	10%	15%
5	$863	$784	$713	$621	$497
10	744	614	508	386	247
15	642	481	362	239	123
20	554	377	258	149	61
25	478	295	184	92	30
30	412	231	131	57	15
35	355	181	94	36	8
40	307	142	67	22	4

payout from your IRA over the years which follow. The first column shows how many years from now you will begin to receive your $1,000 payout beginning five years out and going each five years until forty years later. For example, the first line would refer to a payout that's to begin in five years. The bottom line of the table would refer to a payout that is to begin forty years from now, something which might be apropos to a person twenty-five to thirty years old today.

The next five columns show varying rates of assumed inflation ranging from 3 percent up to 15 percent yearly. Let's start with the most modest rate, 3 percent, in the second column. If you were to receive $1,000 five years from now, but over the interim inflation increased by 3 percent per annum, the purchasing power of that $1,000 five years down the road would be only $863 a month, as seen in the first line of column 2. Continue down column 2 and you would see that in ten years at the inflation rate of 3 percent, your $1,000 today would be worth only $744. The further out you go, the lower the value of your money because of the greater number of years during which inflation erodes your purchasing power. Thus, forty years from now, $1,000 in today's money would be worth only $307.

Now check the fourth column, the one for 7 percent inflation. In the last fifteen years through 1985, inflation in the United States ran at 6.8 percent, roughly that of the 7 percent figure in column 4. Actually, it fell to an average of only 3.9 percent in the last four years of that period, whereas in the first eleven years of that span, it averaged 7.9 percent. On the first line of the 7 percent inflation column, you'll see that five years down the road $1,000 of today's money would be worth only $713. Twenty years later (line 4) the same $1,000 would be worth barely one fourth of the original sum —just $258. Worse, forty years from now, $1,000 of today's money would have a value of only $67, a shockingly small amount if you're planning for retirement.

The next to last column, covering 10 percent inflation, might seem awfully high for the long run, but that's exactly what the inflation rate ran for the five-year period from 1977 through and including 1981. Indeed, it averaged as much as 9.2 percent for a full nine-year span from 1973 through and including 1981. So 10 percent inflation, while quite high for the long run, is nonetheless a possibility based on the experience of the not-too-distant past. Under such grim conditions, your $1,000 today would be worth only $621 in five years or $149 in twenty years. The bottom line of the table shows that forty years from now a $1,000 purchasing power today would buy only $22 worth of goods, a disaster if you are not prepared to cope with the ravages of inflation.

The totally grim news is seen in the final column under 15 percent inflation. We haven't seen any long-run inflation like this in the United States, but numerous countries around the world have had it. Moreover, there is always a chance that we could get involved in a war or some other national calamity for a few years, during which inflation doubles or triples. It may level off after that, but the effects over a twenty- or thirty-year period might average out the inflation at 15 percent. It's a low probability, but it is something you need to concern yourself with. In this truly awful situation, $1,000 of purchasing power is chopped in half in just five years to $497. In ten years it loses over three quarters of its value down to $247. In twenty years your $1,000 is worth only $61, in thirty years $15, and, finally, forty years later $1,000 of purchasing power shrivels to just $4.

In subsequent chapters I will show you how to best overcome this potential inflation obstacle. Moreover, I hope to demonstrate some of the pitfalls and traps into which you might fall if you insist on thinking of "nominal" dollars rather than "real" dollars.

The fact is, a lot of the advertising propaganda for IRAs put out by banks and even by mutual funds shows you how much money you could accumulate at certain rates of interest over a certain time frame . . . and perhaps they'll even translate that into future payouts on a monthly basis. The problem is that these numbers are usually quoted in nominal dollars, ignoring the potential ravages of inflation.

There's nothing much more disheartening than watching an elderly person trying to cope on a limited income which has been severely impaired by heavy inflation, especially when that senior citizen had carefully set aside and invested money and planned for retirement. The budgeted income for later years "appeared" to be sufficient . . . and would have been had there been little or no inflation. But after the steady erosion of purchasing power during some of our recent inflationary periods, a lot of the elderly have suffered on subpar incomes. I don't want to see that happen to you.

CHAPTER 7

CDs—Don't Bank on Them for IRAs

*T*he simple fact about certificates of deposit (CDs) and similar money market instruments such as savings accounts, Treasury bills, or commercial paper is that, historically, their rate of return has been far lower than that of stocks. Today, CDs are yielding much more than their historical average, but that's only been true for several years. Even over that recent time span, CDs have significantly underperformed common stocks. They figure to keep on doing so in the future.

Let's start by looking at the past. As you can see in Table 21, from 1926 through 1985 Treasury bills yielded an average return of 3.5 percent. Data on CDs are not available back to 1926 because these instruments haven't been around that long. CDs did not become significant until the mid-1960s—and even then only in very large denominations for corporations ($100,000 and up). It wasn't until well into the 1970s that smaller CDs first became available to the general public. Had CDs actually existed back to 1926, a reasonable estimate is that they would have yielded roughly .3 percent a year more than Treasury bills, which are somewhat safer. Using that assumption, the long-run average yield on CDs since 1926 would have been 3.8 percent per year.

Note: The risk factor in CDs, while greater than that for Treasury bills, is minimal. Perhaps you might not have felt that way in 1984 had you been an investor in CDs from

TABLE 21

TOTAL RETURNS ON VARIOUS INVESTMENTS
1926 TO 1985

Year	Stocks (S&P 500 Plus Div.)	Long-Term Gov't Bonds (Incl. Int.)	Long-Term Corp. Bonds (Incl. Int.)	U.S. Treasury Bills	Consumer Price Index
1926	+ 11.6%	+ 7.8%	+ 7.4%	+ 3.3%	− 1.5%
1927	+ 37.5	+ 8.9	+ 7.4	+ 3.1	− 2.1
1928	+ 43.6	+ 0.1	+ 2.8	+ 3.2	− 1.0
1929	− 8.4	+ 3.4	+ 3.3	+ 4.8	+ 0.2
1930	− 24.9	+ 4.7	+ 8.0	+ 2.4	− 6.0
1931	− 43.3	− 5.3	− 1.9	+ 1.1	− 9.5
1932	− 8.2	+ 16.8	+ 10.8	+ 1.0	− 10.3
1933	+ 54.0	− 0.1	+ 10.4	+ 0.3	+ 0.5
1934	− 1.4	+ 10.0	+ 13.8	+ 0.2	+ 2.0
1935	+ 47.7	+ 5.0	+ 9.6	+ 0.2	+ 3.0
1936	+ 33.9	+ 7.5	+ 6.7	+ 0.2	+ 1.2
1937	− 35.0	+ 0.2	+ 2.8	+ 0.3	+ 3.1
1938	+ 31.1	+ 5.5	+ 6.1	0.0	− 2.8
1939	− 0.4	+ 5.9	+ 4.0	0.0	− 0.5
1940	− 9.8	+ 6.1	+ 3.4	0.0	+ 1.0
1941	− 11.6	+ 0.9	+ 2.7	+ 0.1	+ 9.7
1942	+ 20.3	+ 3.2	+ 2.6	+ 0.3	+ 9.3
1943	+ 25.9	+ 2.1	+ 2.8	+ 0.4	+ 3.2
1944	+ 19.8	+ 2.8	+ 4.7	+ 0.3	+ 2.1
1945	+ 36.4	+ 10.7	+ 4.1	+ 0.3	+ 2.3
1946	− 8.1	− 0.1	+ 1.7	+ 0.4	+ 18.2
1947	+ 5.7	− 2.6	− 2.3	+ 0.5	+ 9.0
1948	+ 5.5	+ 3.4	+ 4.1	+ 0.8	+ 2.7
1949	+ 18.8	+ 6.5	+ 3.3	+ 1.1	− 1.8
1950	+ 31.7	+ 0.1	+ 2.1	+ 1.2	+ 5.8

(TABLE 21 continued)

TOTAL RETURNS ON VARIOUS INVESTMENTS
1926 TO 1985

Year	Stocks (S&P 500 Plus Div.)	Long-Term Gov't Bonds (Incl. Int.)	Long-Term Corp. Bonds (Incl. Int.)	U.S. Treasury Bills	Consumer Price Index
1951	+24.0%	− 3.9%	− 2.7%	+ 1.5%	+ 5.9%
1952	+18.4	+ 1.2	+ 3.5	+ 1.7	+ 0.9
1953	− 1.0	+ 3.6	+ 3.4	+ 1.8	+ 0.6
1954	+52.6	+ 7.2	+ 5.4	+ 0.9	− 0.5
1955	+31.6	− 1.3	+ 0.5	+ 1.6	+ 0.4
1956	+ 6.6	− 5.6	− 6.8	+ 2.5	+ 2.9
1957	−10.8	+ 7.5	+ 8.7	+ 3.1	+ 3.0
1958	+43.4	− 6.1	− 2.2	+ 1.5	+ 1.8
1959	+12.0	− 2.3	− 1.0	+ 3.0	+ 1.5
1960	+ 0.5	+13.8	+ 9.1	+ 2.7	+ 1.5
1961	+26.9	+ 1.0	+ 4.8	+ 2.1	+ 0.7
1962	− 8.7	+ 6.9	+ 8.0	+ 2.7	+ 1.2
1963	+22.8	+ 1.2	+ 2.2	+ 3.1	+ 1.7
1964	+16.5	+ 3.5	+ 4.8	+ 3.5	+ 1.2
1965	+12.5	+ 0.7	− 0.5	+ 3.9	+ 1.9
1966	−10.1	+ 3.7	+ 0.2	+ 4.8	+ 3.4
1967	+24.0	− 9.2	− 5.0	+ 4.2	+ 3.0
1968	+11.1	− 0.3	+ 2.6	+ 5.2	+ 4.7
1969	− 8.5	− 5.1	− 8.1	+ 6.6	+ 6.1
1970	+ 4.0	+12.1	+18.4	+ 6.5	+ 5.5
1971	+14.3	+13.2	+11.0	+ 4.4	+ 3.4
1972	+19.0	+ 5.7	+ 7.3	+ 3.8	+ 3.4
1973	−14.7	− 1.1	+ 1.1	+ 6.9	+ 8.8
1974	−26.5	+ 4.4	− 3.1	+ 8.0	+12.2
1975	+37.2	+ 9.2	+14.6	+ 5.8	+ 7.0

(TABLE 21 continued)

TOTAL RETURNS ON VARIOUS INVESTMENTS
1926 TO 1985

Year	Stocks (S&P 500 Plus Div.)	Long-Term Gov't Bonds (Incl. Int.)	Long-Term Corp. Bonds (Incl. Int.)	U.S. Treasury Bills	Consumer Price Index
1976	+23.8%	+16.8%	+18.7%	+ 5.1%	+ 4.8%
1977	− 7.2	− 0.7	+ 1.7	+ 5.1	+ 6.8
1978	+ 6.6	− 1.2	− 0.1	+ 7.2	+ 9.0
1979	+18.4	− 1.2	− 4.2	+10.4	+13.3
1980	+32.4	− 4.0	− 2.6	+11.2	+12.4
1981	− 4.9	+ 1.9	− 1.0	+14.7	+ 8.9
1982	+21.4	+40.4	+43.8	+10.5	+ 3.9
1983	+22.5	+ 0.7	+ 4.7	+ 8.8	+ 3.8
1984	+ 6.3	+15.4	+16.4	+ 9.9	+ 4.0
1985	+31.7	+21.3	+30.1	+ 7.5	+ 3.8
Average:	+ 9.8	+ 4.0	+ 4.8	+ 3.5	+ 3.0

Source: *Stocks, Bonds, Bills and Inflation*, 1985 Yearbook. Chicago: Ibbotson Associates, 1985.

the Continental Illinois Bank in Chicago, although ultimately, with some help from the Federal Reserve, the CD investor came out whole. However, there have been cases where CD investors have not been so fortunate.

You can buy a money market fund which invests in CDs from a broad range of banks. Here the risk factor is relatively small because any one bank going sour would be only a tiny fraction of any one portfolio. The money market funds, however, rarely if ever have a maturity date on their portfolio beyond about three months, so the CDs advertised for two, three, and four years are not included in these portfolios. It's more difficult to find an efficient way to buy a diversified portfolio of CDs from a lot of banks. Nonetheless, you can buy CDs at relatively safe, usually large banks. So let's forget about the risk factor and just say that the risk is somewhat higher than T-bills and so is the yield.

How does that 3.8 percent return stack up against stocks? As seen in the table, common stocks over the 1926 to 1985 period produced a total average return of 9.8 percent per year. This figure was derived by taking the appreciation on the Standard & Poor's 500 Index and adding the dividend return each year. Over the long haul, the appreciation and the dividends were roughly equal. That is, you would have made more than 4 percent a year from appreciation and more than 4 percent a year on dividends.

The table shows how the returns varied from year to year. You'll notice in the common stock column that even after the positive effect of dividends is included, there were years in which the stock market investor would have lost money, in some cases lots of money. But there were also years, such as 1982, 1983, and 1985, when the common stock investor enjoyed very substantial returns. The upshot is that the 9.8 percent return on stocks was accompanied by risk.

That risk translates into nineteen years in which the stock market declined. Even during the years when the market was up, there were risks that the returns would vary. For example, suppose you had a hypothetical investment over a ten-year period that produced an average return of 9.8 percent but never showed a negative year. There would still be some risk. For example, year 1 might show a 20 percent profit; year 2, 1 percent; year 3, 15 percent; year 4, 3 percent; and so on. You still have the risk of not knowing what your return will be. That return will vary around the average return, which means in effect that over half the time you're under-performing your long-run expected average.

That's not so much fun when you're expecting 9.8 percent as a long-run average and wind up with a year such as

1984 when you make only 6.3 percent or 1960 when you earn only .5 percent. The worst risk, though, is that of a loss, especially the severe losses as seen in years such as 1930 (− 24.9 percent) and 1931 (− 43.3 percent) or more recently 1973 (− 14.7 percent) and 1974, in which you would have lost 26.5 percent on your money, including dividend returns.

I'm certainly not going to tell you that common stocks are not risky. They clearly are and they are far riskier than certificates of deposit. However, consider the vast difference in returns on the two instruments. Stocks have yielded some 6 percentage points a year more than CDs. Maybe those 6 points don't seem like much, but consider the typical IRA investor who invests $2,000 per year over a thirty-year stretch, what someone in his twenties or thirties might do.

The total investment of $2,000 a year for thirty years is $60,000. When that return is compounded at 3.8 percent a year, the ending value at your retirement time equals $113,000. The 9.8 percent return available on stocks in the past would have compounded to an ending value of about $349,000. In other words, on CDs you would not even have doubled your original investment. Your $60,000 investment returned a total profit of about $53,000. On stocks your $60,000 investment netted about a $289,000 profit. Clearly, it's worth examining the opportunities of the stock market to see whether it's worth the risk to generate much higher potential returns.

Before I go any further you're very likely to point out that the current return on CDs is in excess of 3.8 percent. In 1986, at this writing, the rate hovers around 5.5 to 6 percent. Of course, that's for three-month CDs. You can get somewhat more if you want to stretch the maturities out to a year, two years, three years, or four years. But you'd be locking up your money. And if you think there's virtually no risk with 6 percent CD returns, you might wonder why anyone would want the extra points on stocks badly enough to accept their greater risk.

That's a good point, and if it were so simple, it would be well taken. But the world is much more complex. The future returns on the stock market are not necessarily limited to the 9.8 percent achieved in the past, nor are the current 6 percent CD returns necessarily going to remain the same. In fact, both returns are very likely to change.

In the last couple of years the inflation rate has been running around 3 percent, roughly in line with the long-run inflation rate from 1926 to 1985 (see Table 21). In other words, over the last several decades CDs have returned less than 1 percentage point a year above the inflation rate. Lately they've scored 4 or 5 percentage points more. That is an unstable long-run relationship that is not very likely to hold. Either the inflation rate will go up or the CD rate will go down, or a combination of both might occur.

To keep things simple, assume that the inflation rate remains in the 3 or 4 percent range over the next thirty years (that's just an assumption for this illustration, not a forecast). If so, the CD rate will slowly come down. The CD you buy today, when rolled over several months or a year or two years down the road, will yield a lot less. It is unrealistic to assume that you'll get anywhere near a 6 percent long-run return— say, over a thirty-year period—on CDs, given an inflation rate of 3 or 4 percent.

If the inflation rate stays in the area where it averaged over the past five or six decades, and if the CD rate falls to its more normal level at or around 4 percent, then it would be likely that stocks would return something around their long-run result of 9.8 percent. In other words, we'd be right back at the averages that have held since 1926, where stocks greatly outperformed CDs.

If the traditional pattern holds, the difference in rates of return between CDs and stocks, as shown in Table 22, would have tremendous impact on the totals in your IRA account when you retire. If we assume that CDs yield the

TABLE 22

IMPACT OF DIFFERENT YIELDS
ON IRAs AT RETIREMENT
(Assuming $2,000 investment on the first of each year)

% Rate of Yield	After 5 Years	After 15 Years	After 25 Years	After 35 Years
4	$11,266	$ 41,649	$ 86,623	$ 153,197
5	11,604	43,315	100,227	189,672
6	11,951	49,345	116,313	236,241
7	12,307	53,776	135,353	295,827
8	12,672	58,649	157,909	372,205
9	13,047	64,007	184,648	470,250
10	13,431	69,900	216,364	596,254
11	13,826	76,380	253,998	758,329
12	14,230	83,507	298,668	966,927
13	14,645	91,344	351,700	1,235,500
14	15,071	99,961	414,665	1,581,350
15	15,508	109,435	489,424	2,026,690
16	15,955	119,850	578,176	2,600,050
17	16,414	131,298	683,525	3,337,990
18	16,884	143,878	808,545	4,287,310
19	17,366	157,701	956,862	5,507,840
20	17,860	172,884	1,132,760	7,076,030

traditional 4 percent and stocks 10 percent, your $2,000 annual investment for thirty-five years would leave an ending amount of $153,197 at 4 percent and $596,254 at 10 percent, a whopping difference of $443,057.

Now let's suppose inflation kicks up to, say, 7 percent, which was the case for a good chunk of the past decade. CDs might continue to earn the current 5.5 to 6 percent or possibly somewhat more, although in the long run they've only averaged a percent or so above the inflation rate. If our government were to allow inflation to remain at such a relatively high level of 7 percent over a thirty-year period, the stock market would almost certainly do better than 9.8 percent.

Recall, from Table 21, that stocks have beaten the inflation rate by better than 6 percentage points a year. In a period of higher inflation that gap might narrow somewhat, but it's almost certain to be a positive spread over the long haul.

Graph A shows the year-to-year change in the consumer price index since 1926. The top half of the graph shows the total return on stocks (appreciation plus dividends) on the S&P 500 Index.

So if the inflation rate were to average 7 percent for the next thirty years, it might be reasonable to assume that stocks would return 12 or 13 percent. Their relative advantage over CDs might not be as great as over the past five decades, but it would still be very substantial. The figures in Tables 3, 4, and 5 show the long-term impact of various rates of return.

At this point I should add that, even though common stocks have whipped the inflation rate by more than 6 percentage points in the long run, they are still not a very good hedge against inflationary periods. That may seem puzzling at first glance but here are the facts. Over the years stocks have done their best when inflation has been relatively stable, somewhere in the vicinity of zero to 5 percent, as was true in the huge bull market that began in 1982. The worst returns on common stocks occurred during periods of severe deflation, such as from 1929 to 1933 during the Great Depression. The next worse returns for common stocks were in periods of very rapid inflation.

The reason for this is not so much the inflation itself, which would normally cause most asset prices such as stocks to rise, but rather what the government does or is expected to do to combat the inflation. In fact, when it comes to infla-

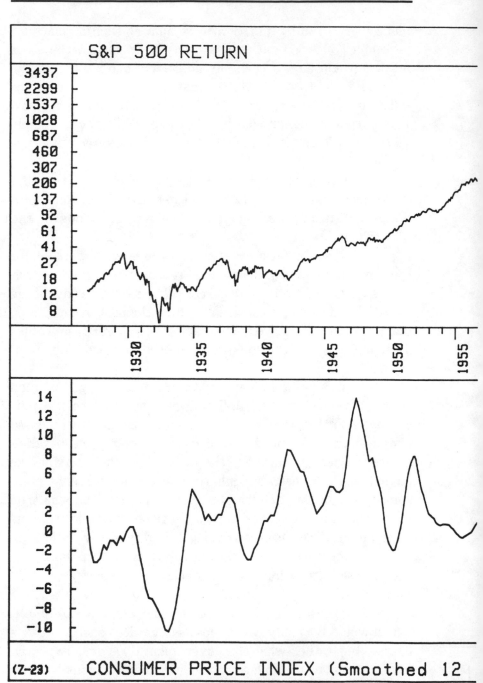

S&P 500 RETURN

(Z-23)   CONSUMER PRICE INDEX (Smoothed 12

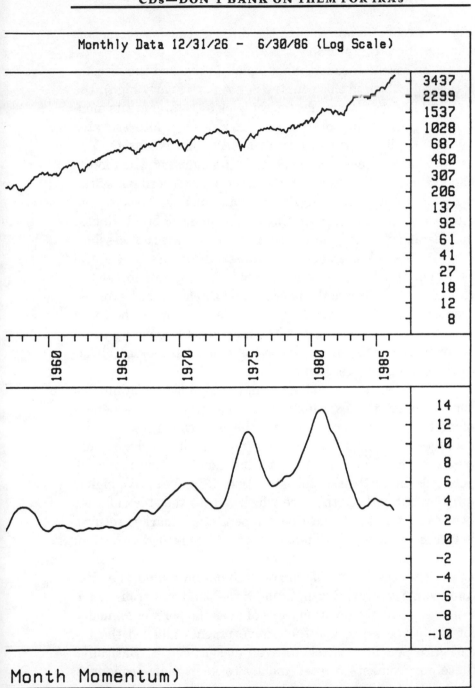

Monthly Data 12/31/26 - 6/30/86 (Log Scale)

3437
2299
1537
1028
687
460
307
206
137
92
61
41
27
18
12
8

1960   1965   1970   1975   1980   1985

14
12
10
8
6
4
2
0
-2
-4
-6
-8
-10

Month Momentum)

tion, the "cure" is worse than the disease, causing recessions and hurting stock prices.

In recent decades, when inflation reached the discomfort level (which in this country is not particularly high), the Federal Reserve Board has fought back by tightening its monetary policy, causing interest rates to rise. Once interest rates go up enough, they tend to throttle economic expansion. You know what happens to the construction industry when mortgage rates soar—potential home buyers are forced out of the market. Other people stop buying automobiles because the interest rate is too high on their installment debt. Business, in general, contracts and we usually wind up with a recession.

The stock market always looks ahead. As it sees the Fed tighten policy and interest rates climb, it anticipates the recession. Stock prices then decline and a bear market evolves. Ironically, the bear market generally ends right in the teeth of the recession and stock prices have usually gone up in its latter phases, this time because the market is looking ahead to the subsequent recovery.

But suppose we adopt a new economic policy in this country over the next thirty years, one that is more benevolent toward inflation. That is, the government would encourage inflation and discourage fighting it. Perhaps, just perhaps, the United States will find that printing money is politically easier than stopping inflation. If so, we'll have higher inflation but without the cure which wrecks the stock market every few years. Should that happen, stock market returns in future years with high inflation would be much greater than in past years.

The possibility of runaway inflation cannot be discounted. Argentina, Brazil, Chile, Israel, and numerous other countries have had inflation rates of over 100 percent annually for many years because their governments allowed the inflation to persist unchecked, even encouraged it. Basically, these governments printed money to keep their economies moving. Politically, they were afraid to stem the growth in money supply or to make the necessary cutbacks because that would have worked even worse short-run hardships on their citizenry.

Presumably, because we are a superpower, the United States would not elect to go that route. However, England and France used to be superpowers and their inflation rates ran a lot higher than ours in the last decade or two. Germany was a superpower before and during World War I, but after the war it unleashed the most devastating inflation known to man. Over a nine-year period ending in 1923, it took billions of marks to buy what just one mark had bought only nine years earlier! It was not until 1923 that Germany decided to bite the bullet and halt the inflation. The government literally stopped printing money. Twenty-three plants had been working around the clock creating currency. When they finally pulled the switch, the inflation ended.

Let's assume we let inflation run rampant and that U.S. inflation over the next thirty years averages 15 percent (just a number I pulled out of the air, again not a prediction). This would certainly imply that the government was not actively combating the inflation, and therefore the Federal Reserve's "cure" would not inhibit stock prices. The market would almost certainly do better than the inflation rate, but let's say by a somewhat narrower spread than in past years. Instead of beating the inflation rate by more than 6 percentage points, suppose the stock market beats it by only 4 percentage points, or 19 percent a year.

Of course we don't know what CD rates would do in that kind of environment. They might beat the inflation rate, they might even lag it. It's hard to say. It depends on the behavior of the government. About the only reasonable assumption is that the stock market would beat the CD rate by a decent spread. Indeed, I might have even grossly underestimated the stock market returns during very heavy inflation. As inflation heats up dramatically, people seek inflation hedges, and buy stocks in oil, timber, mining, and other industries. It's not unusual for such stocks to do far better than the inflation rate as money seeks a haven from the ravages of inflation. In a period of 15 percent long-run inflation, stocks might return 20 to 25 percent a year.

The point is that whatever the future inflation level, low, medium, or high, the stock market is a nearly certain bet to beat the CD rate. That really leaves the risk of fluctuation and occasional down years to deal with. In later chapters I will show you how to dramatically cut that risk inherent in the stock market while actually increasing the return above that of the buy-and-hold investor. If you can curtail the risks, stocks become enormously more attractive than CDs.

CHAPTER 8

Stocks vs. Bonds— Which Are Best for IRAs?

*B*etter-grade bonds offer at least one advantage over stocks: They are less risky. For bonds, the annual total return (interest plus appreciation or depreciation) fluctuates a lot less than that on common stocks (dividends plus appreciation or depreciation). Moreover, for bonds issued by the U.S. Government, the risk of default is almost nil. So the investor has somewhat greater assurance of the revenue stream of interest on his bonds than he would on the assurance of a dividend stream from stocks.

I'm not talking about so-called junk bonds, which are lower than investment-grade bonds. In many cases, these can be riskier than stocks. But if we just talk about U.S. Government securities and the high-grade corporate bonds, those rated AAA, AA, or A by the major rating services such as Moody's and Standard & Poor's, we can safely conclude that bonds are less risky than stocks.

Unfortunately, though, for bond investors, the rates of return realized on bonds over the years have been substantially lower than those received by stock investors. Let's look at the historical returns from 1926 to 1985, a sixty-year span. According to data provided by Ibbotson Associates, U.S. Government bonds produced an average annual return of 4.0 percent, while corporate bonds returned 4.8 percent (see Table 16). Let's assume that you are willing to take the slightly higher risk of corporate bonds versus government bonds in order to capture the extra fraction of a percent return. Even so, the bonds badly lagged the 9.8 percent one could have gotten by buying the Standard & Poor's 500 stock index, including the dividends.

Assuming a continuation of the long-range historic returns, how would you fare with IRA investments in CDs, corporate bonds, and stocks? Well, as you'll see in Table 23, $2,000 invested annually in CDs at 4 percent would give you an ending total of $116,657 in thirty years. Over the same time frame, a like investment in corporate bonds at 5 percent would yield $139,521, while 10 percent in stocks would aggregate $361,887. The 10 percent result achieved in stocks tops CDs by $245,230 and corporate bonds by $222,366.

Over the sixty-year period, 1926–85, a $10,000 investment in common stocks would have become $2.7 million by the end of 1985. A similar $10,000 investment in corporate

TABLE 23

COMPARISON OF ESTIMATED IRA RETURNS ON INVESTMENTS IN STOCKS, BONDS, AND CDs
(Assuming $2,000 investment on the first of each year)

Years	10% Stocks	5% Corp. Bonds	4% CDs
5	13,431	11,604	11,266
10	35,062	26,414	24,973
15	69,900	45,315	41,649
20	126,005	69,439	61,938
25	216,364	100,227	86,623
30	361,887	139,521	116,657
35	596,254	189,672	153,197
40	973,704	253,679	197,653

bonds (which yielded more than the government's) over the sixty years would have had an ending value of only $167,000. Obviously, that's one heck of a difference in gains to give up for the lower risk in bonds. The differences are even more magnified when one considers the inflation rate. Such numbers as rates of return or ending wealth values can be rendered meaningless during periods of significant inflation. Remember when a Coke used to cost a nickel or that you'd get change for a dollar after ordering a meal at McDonald's?

Obviously, the value of money has changed because of inflation. Even the high-flying silver speculator Bunker Hunt once replied, after losing a ten-figure sum in silver bullion, "Well, a billion dollars isn't what it used to be." So we have to remove the rubber yardstick created by inflation.

Over that sixty-year span, the Consumer Price Index in the United States rose at an annualized rate of 3 percent. A $10,000 investment sixty years ago at a 3 percent rate would equal about $59,000 at the end of 1985. To twist it around, $59,000 in today's money was the equivalent of $10,000 sixty years ago. Or, if you prefer, $10,000 today was worth only about $1,700 back in 1926. Rounding out these numbers, $1 sixty years ago is equal to about $6 today, or $1 today was worth about $.17 sixty years back. If you think of $1 today being equal to the dollar of 1926, you are just kidding yourself by comparing apples and oranges. Forgive me, but it's not very fruitful.

In order to adjust for the effects of inflation, we have to subtract the inflation rate from the returns on particular investments. Consider that 4.8 percent long-run rate of return on bonds. If we subtract out the inflation rate, it equals only 1.8 percent "real" return. In other words, after subtracting the ravages of inflation, you would have made a net of only 1.8 percent per year holding corporate bonds over the past sixty years (and only 1.0 percent on the government's) . . . that's before the impact of income taxes. Meanwhile, common stocks produced a nominal return of 9.8 percent. When we subtract the 3 percent inflation rate, we're left with a real return of 6.8 percent. It's proper to compare the historical performance of stocks versus bonds only *after* the inflation rate has been considered. In other words, the real stock return of 6.8 percent is 5 percentage points better than the 1.8 percent real return produced by bonds.

Now, let's compound these *real* returns, assuming a hypothetical $10,000 investment sixty years ago. Such an investment in bonds would have grown to only $29,100 by 1985. On the other hand, a similar $10,000 investment in common stocks would have risen to about $517,900 in sixty years. Thus, the real return in common stocks was greater than that for bonds by a staggering amount. Your total profit on stocks, subtracting the original $10,000 investment, would have been $507,900, while the profit on bonds would have been only about $19,100!

So, would you rather have more than half a million dollars of profits or a mere $19,000? Well, that would have been your actual experience over the past sixty years in stocks versus bonds assuming that you could have replicated either the Standard & Poor's 500 Index of blue chip stocks or a package of high-grade corporate bonds. Looking at history, the odds clearly favor stocks for the investor even if it entails somewhat greater risk to get those returns.

The skeptic might say, though, that in 1986 (at this writing), it's easy to get about a 10 percent return or even more in long-term corporate bonds. Moreover, with the advent of the newfangled Wall Street invention called zero coupon bonds, an investor can guarantee locking in that assumed 10 percent return for the next twenty or even thirty years. That eliminates an uncertainty usually faced by bond investors. For example, if you buy a bond today with a 10 percent current yield, you would receive the interest this year. But at the end of the year, when it comes time to reinvest your money, there's no guarantee that interest rates will still be at 10 percent. Suppose they have fallen to 8 percent. Then your reinvestment rate would be at only 8 percent. You'd have trouble compounding at the original 10 percent return.

The advent of zero coupon bonds has solved this problem. A broker will arrange to make a zero coupon bond out of, say, a twenty-year corporate bond. For a relatively small sum compared with the face value of the bond, you can buy that bond and receive full payment on it thirty years hence. You get no interest along the way. However, the interest is imputed and you buy that bond at a discount to allow for that.

For example, assume a bond has a face value of $1,000, the amount which the corporation will pay you twenty years down the road. If you could buy that bond for approximately $150 today and receive $1,000 for it twenty years hence, your effective compounded annual return would be about 10 percent. So on a twenty-year 10 percent zero coupon bond, you would pay about $150 and get $1,000 back twenty years later.

One of the drawbacks on these bonds for individual investors is that the interest is considered by Uncle Sam to have been received each year, even though it has not been paid. You must therefore pay taxes on the interest even though you do not receive the cash. Obviously, individual tax-paying investors would not want to buy such a bond.

However, in an IRA account where taxes are deferred, zero coupon bonds have become very popular because the tax problem is avoided. The IRA investor could argue that he could lock up a 10 percent or perhaps even greater return on bonds by buying the zero coupon variety. Certainly, the 10 percent you could lock up today is more than double the long-run rate of return produced on bonds over the past sixty years. On the surface, these bonds look like a good bet, even against common stocks.

What could go wrong with these zero coupon bonds, or at least relatively wrong versus the alternative of buying common stocks? Well, let's look at our old nemesis inflation again. For simplicity, let's assume inflation can do one of three things over the next twenty years or so. One, it could be "high," say 7 or 8 percent at a minimum up to any sky-high number you care to pick, say, 20, 30, or even 50 percent. Second, inflation could be "stable," hovering near the zero mark or perhaps plus or minus a couple of percentage points. Third, there could be devastating deflation where price levels actually would decline several percentage points a year over the period.

Let's dismiss the last case very quickly. There have been short-run bouts of deflation such as those in the early 1930s in this country. But the government and the public would in no way stand for long-run deflation. If it ever begins, the Federal Reserve would go all out to expand the money supply (something they failed to do in the early thirties) and quickly pump us out. Politically, there would be far too much pressure brought to bear on the government to combat severe deflation, because deflation would usher in enormous economic problems such as depression and heavy unemployment. High inflation would be a preferable though not a very terrific alternative.

So we might get a few years here and there of deflation, but certainly not a twenty-year period. Stocks would not do well during periods of extreme deflation; high-grade bonds would. But to assume such conditions for the long run is the equivalent of looking for Halley's Comet on a cloudy night. It just isn't going to happen.

Now let's go back to alternative one, very heavy inflation. If you buy that 10 percent zero coupon bond, you are locked in at a 10 percent rate of return. Nowadays, with inflation running around 3 or 4 percent a year, that 10 percent return looks mighty good. But what if inflation were to jump to, say, 15 percent a year for the long run? You would wind up losing 5 percentage points per year after subtracting the inflation rate. Your "real return" would be negative.

Inflation wouldn't even have to be that drastic for you to get rather puny returns. For example, if inflation kicked up to say 8½ percent a year, your real return would be just 1½ percent a year, or a bit less than that of the past sixty years. That's not farfetched. For the decade from 1972 through and including 1981, the Consumer Price Index rose at a compounded annual rate of 8.6 percent, and for the nine years ending 1981 it rose at a 9.2 percent a year clip.

For the ten years through 1981, even though there were, by my reckoning, four bear markets in that span, the average annual return on common stocks was 6.5 percent. That's 2.1 percent a year in "real losses" when compared with inflation. In that time corporate bonds showed profits averaging only 3.0 percent a year in "nominal" terms—for a "real loss" of 5.6 percent a year. So stocks were no barn-burners during that inflationary decade, but they outperformed bonds by 3.5 percent a year and did less poorly against inflation than did bonds.

Now, as I noted in the previous chapter on CDs, in recent decades the government has opted to fight heavy inflation when it rears its head, at least in times of peace. If it continues that policy, we're not very likely to have a very high long-run inflation rate. Inflation might heat up to 10 percent or so for a few years as it did in the late 1970s, but then the government would come in to tighten monetary policy and cool down the inflation rate. As I pointed out previously, should the government not take any action, stocks would do very well during a period of rapid inflation. They would almost certainly beat bonds. If we assumed a long-run inflation rate of 8½ percent, it's highly likely that stocks would beat that mark by several percentage points and produce a "real return" well in excess of your "locked in" zero coupon bond "real return" of 1.5 percent in that environment.

Take a more drastic case. Suppose we allow runaway inflation in the United States of 20 percent a year for the next twenty years. Your zero coupon bonds would produce a real loss to you of 10 percentage points a year, making your ending capital nearly worthless. Suppose that the best common stocks could do in that period would be to equal the inflation rate— probably an underestimate by at least several points. At least you would have preserved your capital with common stocks, although your real return in this hypothetical example would be zero. But you'd have your money.

With bonds you'd have nearly worthless pieces of paper at the end. That was the actual story in Germany in the early 1920s during the greatest inflationary binge in modern history. Stocks lagged the inflation rate somewhat, but the stock investor at least managed to preserve the bulk of his capital during that extraordinary time. But bond investments became utterly worthless as the German mark depreciated by billionsfold.

Now let's take the more reasonable assumption that inflation will run in the more normal range of the 3 percent level seen over the past sixty years. In that case, your zero coupons would provide a real return of 7 percent, a tough bogey for stocks to beat. Now, okay, you say, if inflation is going to remain at the 3 percent rate we've seen in the past, then perhaps the returns on stocks will hover about the same, namely 9.8 percent a year. That, by my arithmetic, is slightly less than the 10 percent return locked in on zero coupon bonds. True enough, I'll concede, on your investment in year one; but what about your IRA investment in years two, three, four, and so on?

If inflation were to remain at 3 percent every year for the next twenty years, interest rates available on bonds would undoubtedly drop. Recall that in the past bonds provided a return of only about 1½ percent above the inflation rate. It is absurd to assume that bond prices would stay so low that the yield on the bonds would remain at a 10 percent rate while inflation is only 3 percent. That 7 percent real return would be enormously high and unsustainable. As people perceived that inflation would indeed remain low, they would buy bonds, drive their prices up, and hammer the interest rates down.

Let's say in year two the prevailing interest rate went down to 9 percent. You could buy a nineteen-year zero coupon bond but you would only lock in a 9 percent return or .8 percent less than our assumed long-run return on stocks. In year three, as inflation continues to be stable, let's assume that bond yields are now down to 8 percent. You could then buy an eighteen-year zero coupon bond but now you're running about 1.8 percentage points less than the expected return on stocks.

As the trend continues, pretty soon bond prices would be down to a yield of about 4.8 percent to stay in line with that of history. Your average return for the period would be far less than 10 percent but somewhat more than 4.8 percent. Let's average it out at 6 percent. With an inflation rate of 3 percent, that would give you a real return on bonds of 3 percent, or about two-thirds more than that of the past sixty years. That's not bad, but it's still not up to snuff versus stocks. Then, too, I have probably been somewhat liberal in estimating the return on bonds under these conditions. It's more likely to average something less than my 6 percent example.

Summing up, there are three possible major inflation rate trends. Number one, there could be extreme inflation, a condition in which stocks would vastly outperform bonds; bonds could even be devastated if inflation were to go high enough. Possibility two is for relatively stable inflation, where stocks would still beat bonds, as they did in the period from 1926 to 1985. Possibility three is for extreme deflation, in which bonds would theoretically cream stocks. However, the probability of that happening in the long run in the United States is virtually nil. You'd best forget about it as a likely possibility.

As we realistically look at the comparisons of stocks and bonds, keeping inflation in mind, the expected future returns on stocks will clearly surpass those on bonds in the long run. The only burning question is whether the risk that stock investing entails is worth taking on. Sometimes the higher return is not worth the extra risk; other times it is. This is a question that most investors have to answer for themselves.

Some people have high risk tolerances and are willing to suffer through down years and very bad years in order to achieve a higher long-run rate of return. A typical thirty- or forty-year-old successful business person making a large income might perhaps fall into this category. A second type of investor is very risk-averse and demands extreme safety. This group includes the proverbial widows and orphans of the investment world.

There are some very sophisticated ways of measuring risk and comparing the return per unit of risk that you could get on an investment. But measures of risk can often be very theoretical, and conclusions of such studies are not always apropos for the individual investor. My feeling, though, is that an IRA investor has a very long time horizon and very little need for liquidity in the investment along the way. Under such conditions, the IRA investor can afford to take on somewhat greater risk of variability in the year-to-year return than he might otherwise.

I'm not talking about the risk of losing all of one's money, mind you. I'm merely considering the fact that in the stock market you might hit a down year where you could lose 15 to 20 percent of your capital. Of course you could lose money in bonds too in a given year, but not usually as much as in stocks. Nor would you lose in as many years in the long run in bonds as you would in stocks. But since stocks have such higher long-run rates of returns than bonds, it is probably appropriate for most IRA investors to go into stocks.

Suppose I can show you a way to reduce the normal risk in stocks, by cutting it in half, but leaving returns the same or even greater. If you could do that, you could eliminate most or all of the down years in the stock market. If you could lower risk enough, your vulnerability might even wind up being less than that in bonds, in which case stocks would be clearly the superior investment even after risk adjustment. I intend to show you how to do this in subsequent chapters.

CHAPTER 9

Of Prime Concern—
The IRA Monetary Indicator

*I*f there are any two rules in the stock market about which I am adamant, they are "Don't fight the Fed" and "Don't fight the tape." With these rules in mind, I've strived to construct a very simple stock market timer which the novice investor —even the first-time investor—can use to play the stock market in a very conservative way, stay out of trouble, and easily keep up to date with the most important market conditions.

This timer uses just two indicators: monetary and price. Obviously, when I manage money, I use far more than two indicators in my work. But if I attempted to explain to you everything I use, I would probably fill an encyclopedia and bore you to death long before you got through the third or fourth chapter. I think that by simplifying the entire structure, but yet keeping the basic idea intact, I can create a model just for you which works very well. Here goes.

I'm going to develop two indicators with which we will follow the stock market. If both of the indicators are positive, we'll assume that you buy either no-load mutual funds or a portfolio of stocks. When just one of the two indicators turns bearish, we'll move out of the no-load funds or stocks and put the money into money market funds. Obviously, if both indicators are negative, we'll remain in money market funds.

In other words, *both* of our indicators have to be bullish before we'll play the stock market. This is about as conservative as you can get. Occasionally, you'll miss some rallies, but it will be worth it because of the simplicity of the model and the fact that most novice investors, especially with IRA money, are risk-averse. Demanding that both indicators be positive before we buy will also keep the number of transactions to a minimum.

Generally speaking, the monetary environment is the dominant factor in whether stocks flourish or fade. The market's major direction depends in large part on the trend in interest rates and in Federal Reserve policy, which are intertwined. The earlier you spot and trail along with this trend, which usually continues for from one to three years, the better off you'll be.

Several major factors combine to produce a trend in interest rates. These include liquidity in the banking system, loan demand, inflation or deflation, and the Federal Reserve Board policy decisions based on these financial considerations. In the monetary climate, a rising interest rate trend typically foreshadows stormy clouds ahead for stocks while a declining trend portends a more sunny outlook. In this chapter I'll show you how to forecast your own financial weather conditions.

Since stocks are always in competition with other investment vehicles, they benefit when yields decline on certificates of deposits, money market funds, and Treasury bills. When your 12 percent CD comes up for renewal and the bank is only offering 7 percent, you're likely to consider alternate investments rather than locking in your CDs for another fixed period. However, if bank interest rates are rising, you'll have less temptation to switch into other riskier but conceivably more rewarding instruments.

Corporate profits are also linked to the trend in interest rates. Lower rates mean less expensive borrowing and consequently higher net earnings. This is especially true for industries such as airlines, public utilities, and savings and loans, which tend to borrow heavily. Since investors tend to favor companies with anticipated higher earnings, these stocks generally wend higher as interest rates decline. Of course, rising interest rates have the opposite effect.

To chart this all-important interest rate trend, I'll describe the simplest indicator I use. Easy to keep up, it is also extremely effective.

PRIME RATE INDICATOR

The interest rate that banks charge solid major corporations and other favored customers is known as the prime rate. This is the rate against which other bank loans are computed, based on the perceived risk. The degree at which borrowers are deemed creditworthy determines how much above the prime rate they must pay.

Because it changes so infrequently, the prime rate is especially convenient to use as an indicator. During the twenty-one years through April 1986, the prime rate changed an average of 11.1 times a year, slightly less than once a month. And it's hard to miss prime rate movements. They are always headlined in newspaper financial sections and invariably make the TV and radio newscasts as well.

Another feature of the prime rate as an indicator is that it lags other interest rates. Declines in federal funds rates, CDs, and commercial paper usually precede a drop in the prime rate. That's a plus because interest rate changes generally *lead* changes in stock market trends. Therefore, the prime, being just a tad later, frequently pinpoints the time when stocks actually start to react to the rate changes. (You'll find prime rate movements plotted against the Dow Jones Industrial Average in Graph B.)

Here are the basic rules for the Prime Rate Indicator:

Ranges: In setting up my prime rate indicator I determined, somewhat arbitrarily, that a prime rate of 8 percent

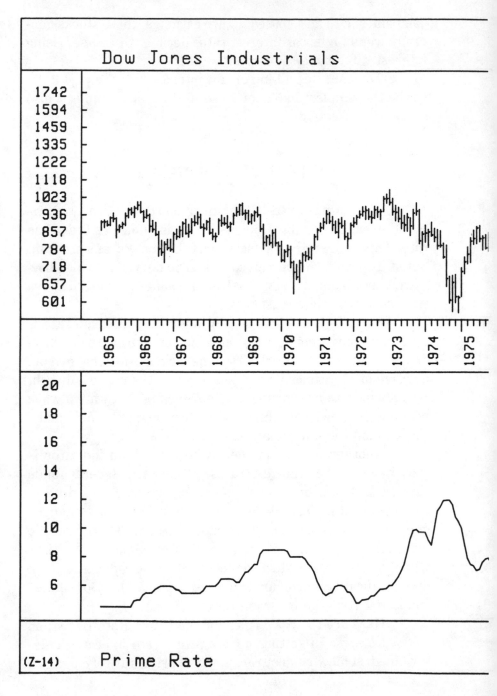

Dow Jones Industrials

(Z-14) Prime Rate

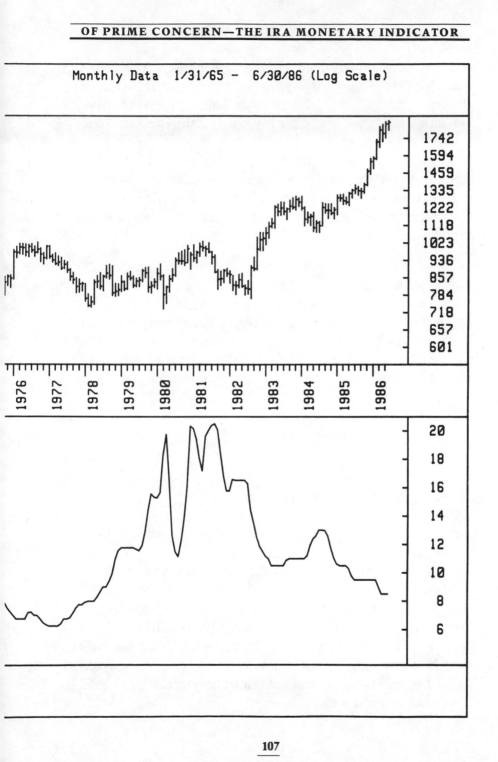

Monthly Data 1/31/65 – 6/30/86 (Log Scale)

or above is relatively high while a figure below 8 percent is relatively low. Consequently, in measuring the impact of declines on stocks, small dips in rates below 8 percent give a bullish signal; larger drops are necessary if the cuts come from above the 8 percent level.

The reverse is true for bearish signals. If rates are above 8 percent, greater increases are needed to signal a bearish trend than if levels are below 8 percent. It really isn't very complicated, as you'll see in the following buy and sell signal examples.

Buy Signals

(a). If the prime's peak is less than 8 percent, a buy signal occurs with an initial cut in the rate. Let's say the prime has climbed gradually from 6 to 7½ percent over a period of months. Finally it is cut to 7 percent, setting off a buy signal for the indicator. Here's how it looks in tabular form:

	Prime Rate
1.	6%
2.	6½%
3.	7½%
4.	7% (Buy signal on initial cut)

(b). The rule is different if the prime's peak is 8 percent or higher. Here, for a buy signal, you need either a full 1 percent cut in the rate or two consecutive drops of any amount. For example, suppose the prime has advanced from 8½ to 9 percent and is then reduced to 8½ percent. That's not sufficient for a buy signal. Assume it is later cut again to 8 percent. That's the necessary second cut which flashes the buy signal. In tabular form, it looks this way:

Prime Rate

1. 8½%
2. 9%
3. 8½% (Not sufficient for signal)
4. 8% (Buy signal on second cut)

Note: Had the first reductions been a full point to 8 percent, that would have been the buy signal. Historically, the prime rate has moved by a full point only one in twenty cases; changes are usually ¼ or ½ percent.

Sell Signals

(a). If the prime's low is 8 percent or higher, a sell signal comes with any initial boost in the rate. Let's say the prime has declined a couple of times from 11 to 10 percent and is then raised to 10½ percent. This indicates a sell signal. In tabular form:

Prime Rate

1. 11%
2. 10½%
3. 10%
4. 10½% (Sell signal on initial hike)

(b). If the prime's low is under 8 percent, a sell signal occurs on the second of two rises or a full 1 percent advance in the rate. Say the prime dips from 7 to 6½ percent and is then raised to 7 percent again. That's not enough for a signal. Then it is boosted to 7½ percent, a second increase and a sell signal. In tabular form:

Prime Rate

1. 7%
2. 6½%
3. 7% (Not sufficient for signal)
4. 7½% (Sell signal on second rise)

TABLE 24

PRIME RATE INDICATOR VS. ZWEIG UNWEIGHTED PRICE INDEX 1954 TO 1986

BUY SIGNALS			**SELL SIGNALS**		
Date	ZUPI	% Change	Date	ZUPI	% Change
3/17/54	33.73	+43.2%	10/14/55	48.29	− 1.3%
1/22/58	47.66	+57.2	5/18/59	74.93	− 1.6
8/23/60	73.74	+70.1	3/10/66	125.43	− 3.3
1/26/67	121.28	+20.8	4/19/68	146.45	+12.2
9/25/68	164.98	+ 7.7	12/02/68	177.68	−42.7
9/21/70	101.86	+21.9	7/06/71	124.17	− 6.1
10/20/71	116.59	+ 3.8	6/26/72	121.02	−34.6
1/29/74	79.17	+ 2.2	3/22/74	80.95	−33.5
10/21/74	53.83	+31.0	7/28/75	70.53	− 5.6
11/05/75	66.59	+20.1	6/07/76	79.95	+ 6.1
8/02/76	84.79	+ 8.0	5/31/77	91.57	+21.2
12/07/79	110.96	+ 5.5	2/19/80	117.09	−11.4
5/01/80	103.73	+27.3	8/26/80	132.08	+ 0.6
12/22/80	132.87	+11.7	4/24/81	148.46	+ 0.9
6/16/81	149.84	− 0.5	6/22/81	149.02	−14.7
9/21/81	127.04	+ 1.3	2/01/82	128.68	− 5.9
3/08/82	121.07	− 0.1	3/16/82	120.96	+ 2.8
7/26/82	124.39	+61.2	8/10/83	200.53	− 3.0
10/15/84*	194.61	+46.1			

$10,000 became: $389,421 $2,164
Annualized return: +23.0%   −10.0%
Buy-and-hold return: 6.9% per year
Percentage of signals correct: 89%   67%

*On May 9, 1986, the indicator was still on a buy signal and the ZUPI stood at 284.28.

Note: If the first advance had been a full point, to 7½ percent, it would have flashed a sell signal.

You can gauge the efficacy of this simple Prime Rate Indicator by looking at Table 24, which shows the indicator's performance from 1954 to 1986 tested against my Zweig Unweighted Price Index (ZUPI), a market average that gives equal weight to all issues listed in the New York Stock Exchange. The Zweig Index's movements are very similar to those of the Value Line Composite Index, calculated by Arnold Bernhard & Co., an unweighted price index of approximately seventeen hundred stocks against which you can trade stock index futures.

Graph C shows the ZUPI and the Value Line Index back to 1965. As you can see, they are very similar. Indeed, you can think of them as almost the same. But over the years I've done an enormous amount of indicator testing against my own price index and I didn't want to change in midstream. Obviously, any tests against the Value Line Index—which is widely available to investors (in daily newspapers and Quotron machines)—would produce nearly identical results.

As you'll see in Table 24, the first buy signal occurred in March 1954, when the ZUPI stood at 33.73. Nineteen months later, in October 1955, the indicator gave a sell signal, as seen on the right side of the table. By then, the ZUPI had advanced to 48.29. The percentage gain on the buy signal was 43.2, shown in the "% Change" column under "Buy Signals."

Following the 1955 sell signal, the Prime Rate Indicator remained bearish until January 1958, when it flashed the second buy signal listed in the table. At that point, the ZUPI had declined to 47.66, 1.3 percent below the level at the 1955 sell signal. You'll note the figure in the first entry on the far-right column under "% Change" for "Sell Signals." The rest of the table can be followed easily.

A total of nineteen buy signals have been given by the indicator, with the last one still "on" at this writing. Sixteen

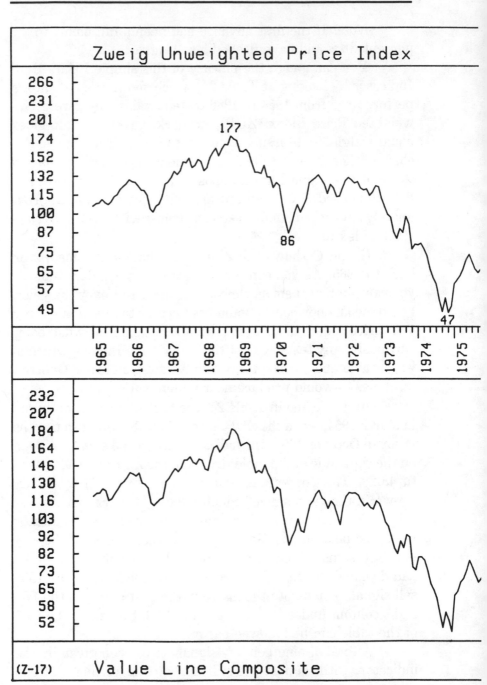

Zweig Unweighted Price Index

(Z-17) Value Line Composite

Monthly Data 1/31/65 - 6/30/86 (Log Scale)

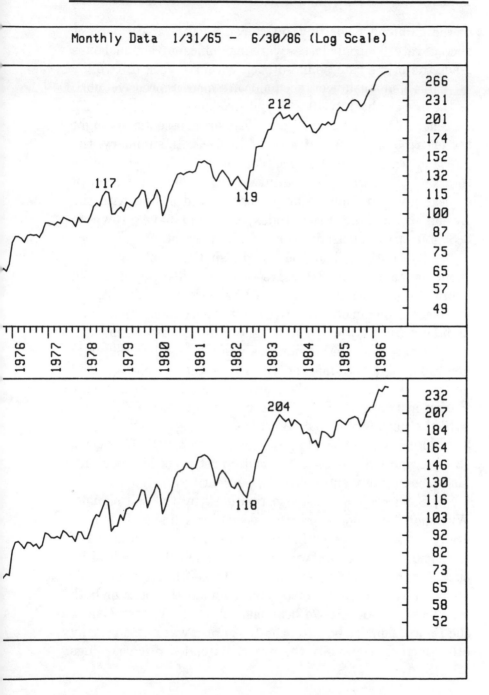

of the eighteen prior buys produced profits, an 89 percent success rate. The only losses were insignificant fractional ones when the prime rate bounced back within a week or two.

In some instances, the gains are most impressive, such as the one on the July 1982 buy; it produced a whopping 61.2 percent profit in just over a year. That signal essentially caught the entire bull market advance of 1982–83. In summary, the indicator was in its bullish position (or mode) for a cumulative total of 17.7 years. Had you invested $10,000 in a basket of typical stocks or mutual funds that moved in line with the Zweig Unweighted Price Index, it would have grown to $389,421, an annualized return of 23.0 percent.

By contrast, had you bought similar stocks and held them constantly for 32.1 years—the so-called buy-and-hold approach—your $10,000 take would have risen to only $84,281, an annualized gain of only 6.9 percent. These calculations, and all others except where noted, ignore dividends and taxes.

Let's take the possibilities one step further. Suppose you had bought the "market" (ZUPI) on the buy signals, sold on the sell signals, and then invested in short-term money market instruments like CDs at an average rate of 7 percent until the next buy signal. With that strategy, your original $10,000 investment would have zoomed to $1,047,075 over a 32.1-year period! That's an annualized return of 15.6 percent, far exceeding buy-and-hold's 6.9 percent.

Solid results were also produced by the sell signals. With monetary indicators, the record for sell signals is generally not as good as with buy signals. However, a dozen of the eighteen sell signals "worked"—prices fell. That's a healthy success average of 67 percent. (See Table 24, bottom line.)

Moreover, you would have avoided the bulk of both the 1969–70 and 1973–74 bear markets, the two worst since the Depression. To be sure, the 1962 crash was missed (many other factors, especially the overly extended price/earnings

TABLE 25

PRIME RATE INDICATOR VS. STANDARD & POOR'S 500 INDEX 1954 TO 1986

BUY SIGNALS			SELL SIGNALS		
Date	S&P	% Change	Date	S&P	% Change
3/17/54	26.62	+54.8%	10/14/55	41.22	0.0%
1/22/58	41.20	+41.1	5/18/59	58.15	− 0.7
8/23/60	57.75	+54.0	3/10/66	88.96	− 3.5
1/26/67	85.81	+11.7	4/19/68	95.85	+ 6.8
9/25/68	102.36	+ 5.6	12/02/68	108.12	−24.2
9/21/70	81.91	+21.8	7/06/71	99.76	− 4.1
10/20/71	95.65	+12.4	6/26/72	107.48	−10.7
1/29/74	96.01	+ 1.3	3/22/74	97.27	−24.4
10/21/74	73.50	+20.7	7/28/75	88.69	− 0.5
11/05/75	89.15	+10.6	6/07/76	98.63	+ 4.6
8/02/76	103.19	− 6.9	5/31/77	96.12	+11.9
12/07/79	107.52	+ 6.6	2/19/80	114.60	− 8.0
5/01/80	105.46	+18.4	8/26/80	124.84	+ 8.8
12/22/80	135.78	− 0.5	4/24/81	135.14	− 2.2
6/16/81	132.15	− 0.2	6/22/81	131.95	−11.1
9/21/81	117.24	+ 0.5	2/01/82	117.78	− 8.9
3/08/82	107.34	+ 1.8	3/16/82	109.28	+ 1.0
7/26/82	110.36	+46.4	8/10/83	161.54	− 2.6
10/15/84*	165.77	+43.5			

$10,000 became: $184,221 $4,854
Annualized return: +17.9%   − 4.9%
Buy-and-hold return: 7.1% per year
Percentage of signals correct: 83%   59%

*On May 9, 1986, the indicator was still on a buy signal and the S&P stood at 237.85.

ratios, were terrible then), but the more recent 1980 and 1981 downturns were nailed.

If, unfortunately, you had ignored the warnings of rising interest rates and insisted on holding stocks during the "sell modes" (the intervals from sell signals to the next buy signal), your $10,000 investment would have shriveled to only $2,164, an annualized loss rate of 10.0 percent.

A similar test of the Prime Rate Indicator against the Standard & Poor's 500 Index (a composite of five hundred blue chip stocks) is shown in Table 25. Not as volatile as the ZUPI, the S&P will virtually never provide returns on an indicator as good as those on the ZUPI. The S&P test reveals gains on the buy signals of 17.9 percent compared with buy-and-hold of only 7.1 percent. Had you gone into money market instruments in the sell modes and achieved an average yield of 7 percent, your $10,000 investment would have appreciated to $495,333, a respectable 12.9 percent annualized gain, close to double that of buy-and-hold.

The S&P went up fifteen times in eighteen tries on the buy signals, a success rate of 83 percent. On the sell signals, the S&P 500 fell ten times, stayed even once, and rose seven times. That's equivalent to a 59 percent batting average. A "wrong way" investor would have seen his $10,000 stake dwindle to $4,854 during the sell modes, a loss of 4.9 percent per annum.

As you can see, the Prime Rate Indicator, based on monetary considerations, is a valuable stock market trend forecasting tool. The same holds true for our price guidepost, the Four Percent Model Indicator, described in the next chapter.

CHAPTER 10

The Price Is Right—
The IRA Tape Indicator

*O*ur composite stock market timer consists of two major components: the Prime Rate Indicator, discussed in the previous chapter, and the Four Percent Model Indicator, which will be covered in this chapter.

Simply speaking, the Four Percent Model Indicator measures the broad spectrum of stock market prices. This is possible because every transaction in the market is recorded electronically with the name of the stock, the price of the trade, and the volume. Years ago this information was actually printed out on ticker tape, which is why the activity of the market itself is called tape action—and our indicator could also be called the Tape Indicator.

Although the tape encompasses price and volume, price is a more important variable, so we'll focus on the price action. Price indexes include the Dow Jones Industrial Average, the Standard & Poor's 500 Index, the Value Line Composite Index, and my unweighted index, the ZUPI.

It is not always easy to decide on the significance of the tape action. Things may not be what they seem. For example, is it always true that if the Dow Jones Average goes up by a certain percentage, it's bullish, and that if it declines by a similar percentage, it's bearish? Sounds obvious but it ain't necessarily so. Some observers might contend that the market has risen so far that it's overbought and likely to drop. Or, if the average is down significantly, it could be argued that the market is oversold and poised to rise.

This raises the key question: Does market strength tend to beget strength, or does strength tend to wane and lead to weakness? After years of testing market averages, advance/decline ratios, volume figures, and other indicators, I have found that strength does tend to lead to greater strength and, conversely, that weakness leads to more weakness. An easy way to remember this market pattern is embodied in an expression I like to use: *The trend is your friend.* The following indicator is designed to keep you in tandem with the trend.

THE FOUR PERCENT MODEL INDICATOR

Of course no indicator is right all the time. In fact, the tape indicator I am about to explain is right only about half the time. But, more important, the profits derived from following it are excellent.

The Four Percent Model was developed by Ned Davis, a close friend and colleague. Davis edits three market letters I publish: *Futures Hotline*, which covers stock index futures, interest rate futures, foreign currencies, and precious metals; *Business Timing Guide*, which calls the direction of the economy and the inflation rate; and our newest service, the *Bond Fund Timer*, which gives advice on when to switch from bond mutual funds to money funds. A simplified version of the bond timer model we use is described in Chapter 12.

Here's how the Four Percent Model works. First, it uses the Value Line Composite Index, which, you'll recall, is an unweighted average of about seventeen hundred stocks. This index is listed in the financial pages of your newspaper or in *Barron's*. It is also reported regularly on Quotron machines. We selected the Value Line Index for this model because it is readily available and easy to follow.

To construct this model, you only need *the weekly close of the Value Line Composite.* You'll find this figure in your Saturday or Sunday newspaper or in *Barron's*, which arrives on the newsstands on Saturday. This trend-following model flashes a buy signal when the weekly Value Line Index climbs 4 percent or more from any weekly close. A sell signal is given when the weekly close drops 4 percent or more from any weekly peak. *Important: To obtain a signal, you need 4 percent of change, not four points.*

Let's look at an example. If the Value Line Index closes at 200 in the first week, it would take a reading of at least 208 to give a buy signal. Assume that happens in a week when the Value Line Index closes at 209. The buy signal holds as long as there is no 4 percent or greater drop in the weekly Value Line Index.

Suppose the Value Line continues to rally, possibly with small dips along the way—none of which are greater than 4 percent—until it attains a weekly closing high of 240. At that point, suppose the index begins to fall. It would have to drop by 4 percent, or to a level of 230.40 or less, to generate a sell signal. Let's say that happens in a week when the Value Line closes at 229. The sell point would be 229, and the model would stay on the sell signal until after there was a rally of 4 percent or greater.

It's that simple. If you can spare a few minutes a week and have a calculator (or remember your long division), you can construct the Four Percent Model and keep it up to date with a minimum of effort.

As you will see, this model was designed to keep you in line with the market trend. Significant moves on the upside and downside will automatically give buy or sell signals. The only potential problem is that you are using weekly data and the market may move by more than 4 percent before you get a change in signals. Should the market make a big move in any given week, you may buy at 6 or 7 or 8 percent above a weekly low, or perhaps sell at that much below a weekly high. But that doesn't happen very often and, in any case, you're in step with the major trend.

Although you are guaranteed of being on the right side of major moves, you may get whipsawed over very short-term movements. If the market were to hem and haw by moves only a little bit greater than 4 percent, you might be hemming when you should be hawing and hawing when you should be hemming. But that's all part of the game. It may cost you some money from time to time, but the long-term results of the Four Percent Model clearly show that it is worth that cost.

All the signals from Davis's test of the Four Percent Model, beginning with May 1966, are shown in Table 26, together with the financial results. In calculating the results, we have assumed that you sell short on the sell signals and go long on the buy signals. Now, I don't necessarily advise that you do that, but I want to show what the profits would have been had you sold the market short on the sell signals.

The percentage of profit on all of the signals, both the sells and the buys, is shown in the fourth column of the table. The fifth column shows the number of calendar days during which each signal was open, and the final column gives a running total of the cumulative value of an initial $10,000 portfolio.

I should point out that the results are theoretical because no one could have bought and sold the Value Line Index over this period. Stock index futures began to trade on the Value Line Index in 1982. Since that date, you could have closely approximated the results shown. From 1966 to 1982, you could have approximated the results by buying diversified mutual funds with broad-based portfolios or by buying a di-

TABLE 26

FOUR PERCENT MODEL VS. VALUE LINE COMPOSITE INDEX MAY 6, 1966, TO APRIL 12, 1985

Signal	Date	Value Line Index	% Profit	Days	$10,000 Growth
Sell	5/06/66	133.09	+ 15.9%	168	$11,591
Buy	10/21/66	111.92	+ 33.6	371	15,488
Sell	10/27/67	149.55	− 2.2	63	15,142
Buy	12/29/67	152.89	− 4.5	42	14,463
Sell	2/09/68	146.04	+ 0.3	56	14,510
Buy	4/05/68	145.57	+ 12.3	112	16,300
Sell	7/26/68	163.53	− 2.9	42	15,831
Buy	9/06/68	168.24	+ 5.2	126	16,653
Sell	1/10/69	176.98	+ 3.1	119	17,172
Buy	5/09/69	171.46	− 8.0	35	15,798
Sell	6/13/69	157.74	+ 8.3	126	17,114
Buy	10/17/69	144.60	− 3.2	35	16,564
Sell	11/21/69	139.95	+ 8.8	105	18,022
Buy	3/06/70	127.63	− 4.6	14	17,192
Sell	3/20/70	121.75	+ 21.7	70	20,198
Buy	5/29/70	95.36	− 6.9	28	19,475
Sell	6/26/70	88.78	− 1.9	21	19,100
Buy	7/17/70	90.49	− 3.7	28	18,458
Sell	8/14/70	87.45	− 9.3	14	16,742
Buy	8/28/70	95.58	+ 2.0	56	17,082
Sell	10/23/70	97.52	− 1.4	42	16,837
Buy	12/04/70	98.92	+ 19.6	175	10,130
Sell	5/28/71	118.27	+ 3.5	84	20,843
Buy	8/20/71	114.08	− 2.2	56	20,381
Sell	10/15/71	111.55	+ 5.1	49	21,410
Buy	12/03/71	105.92	+ 13.2	154	24,236
Sell	5/05/72	119.90	+ 6.2	189	25,741
Buy	11/10/72	112.45	+ 0.6	42	25,899
Sell	12/22/72	113.14	+ 25.3	203	32,460
Buy	7/13/73	84.48	+ 1.6	28	32,986

(TABLE 26 continued)

FOUR PERCENT MODEL VS.
VALUE LINE COMPOSITE INDEX
MAY 6, 1966, TO APRIL 12, 1985

Signal	Date	Value Line Index	% Profit	Days	$10,000 Growth
Sell	8/10/73	85.85	− 1.2%	28	$32,595
Buy	9/07/73	86.87	+ 3.6	56	33,754
Sell	11/02/73	89.96	+12.1	63	37,821
Buy	1/04/74	79.12	− 0.9	84	37,501
Sell	3/29/74	78.45	+ 9.1	70	40,914
Buy	6/07/74	71.31	− 6.5	14	38,263
Sell	6/21/74	66.69	+20.2	91	46,003
Buy	9/20/74	53.20	− 6.3	14	43,115
Sell	10/04/74	49.86	−11.8	7	38,039
Buy	10/11/74	55.73	− 5.5	42	35,957
Sell	11/22/74	52.68	+ 1.1	42	36,940
Buy	1/03/75	52.12	+45.2	203	52,766
Sell	7/25/75	75.68	+ 5.8	112	55,813
Buy	11/14/75	71.31	− 5.0	21	53,109
Sell	12/05/75	67.74	− 5.7	28	49,982
Buy	1/02/76	71.62	+19.7	98	59,808
Sell	4/09/76	85.70	− 1.4	77	58,992
Buy	6/25/76	86.87	− 1.3	56	58,245
Sell	8/20/76	85.77	− 2.8	35	56,629
Buy	9/24/76	88.15	− 4.1	14	54,309
Sell	10/08/76	84.54	− 2.3	49	53,044
Buy	11/26/76	86.51	+ 4.0	133	55,159
Sell	4/08/77	89.96	− 5.5	77	52,130
Buy	6/24/77	94.90	− 3.1	56	50,493
Sell	8/19/77	91.92	− 0.5	84	50,263
Buy	11/11/77	92.34	− 1.5	56	49,517
Sell	1/06/78	90.97	− 3.4	70	47,813
Buy	3/17/78	94.10	+10.6	105	52,899
Sell	6/30/78	104.11	− 4.5	28	50,496
Buy	7/28/78	108.84	+ 4.4	56	52,718
Sell	9/22/78	113.63	+11.8	77	58,944
Buy	12/08/78	100.21	+14.9	308	67,738

(TABLE 26 continued)

FOUR PERCENT MODEL VS.
VALUE LINE COMPOSITE INDEX
MAY 6, 1966, TO APRIL 12, 1985

Signal	Date	Value Line Index	% Profit	Days	$10,000 Growth
Sell	10/12/79	115.16	+ 1.3%	42	$68,626
Buy	11/23/79	113.65	+ 9.6	98	75,178
Sell	2/29/80	124.50	+11.5	42	83,801
Buy	4/11/80	110.20	+29.3	210	108,321
Sell	11/07/80	142.47	− 4.1	7	103,926
Buy	11/14/80	148.25	− 7.3	28	96,313
Sell	12/12/80	137.39	− 5.0	14	91,483
Buy	12/26/80	144.28	+ 4.9	196	96,004
Sell	7/10/81	151.41	+12.3	84	107,810
Buy	10/02/81	132.79	− 0.8	105	107,007
Sell	1/15/82	131.80	+ 3.1	77	110,278
Buy	4/02/82	127.77	− 2.3	56	107,784
Sell	5/28/82	124.88	+ 2.9	84	110,857
Buy	8/20/82	121.32	+64.3	343	182,184
Sell	7/29/83	199.38	− 1.6	56	179,279
Buy	9/23/83	202.56	− 4.2	28	171,791
Sell	10/21/83	194.10	− 1.7	35	168,959
Buy	11/25/83	197.30	− 4.4	70	161,568
Sell	2/03/84	188.67	+ 6.0	182	171,305
Buy	8/03/84	177.30	− 0.9	119	169,837
Sell	11/30/84	175.78	− 3.0	42	164,716
Buy	1/11/85	181.08	+ 7.2	91	176,596

versified portfolio of stock heavily weighted toward medium- and smaller-sized companies.

The buy and sell signals on the Four Percent Model plotted against the Value Line Index back to 1978 are shown in Graph D. The "B's" on the graph show the buy signals while the "S's" show the sell signals.

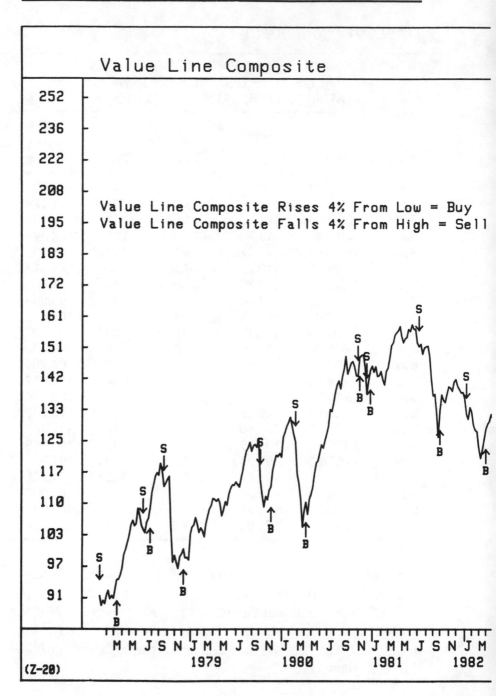

Value Line Composite

Value Line Composite Rises 4% From Low = Buy
Value Line Composite Falls 4% From High = Sell

(Z-20)

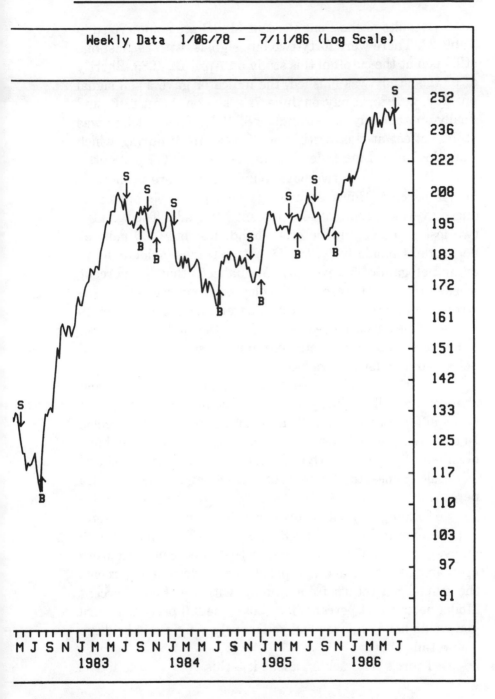

Weekly Data 1/06/78 - 7/11/86 (Log Scale)

Results of the Four Percent Model are summarized in Table 27. There were forty-two buy signals, with the last one still open at the cutoff of this study on April 12, 1985. Shortly after this study was finished, the indicator gave a sell signal on May 3, 1985, a buy on June 7, a sell on August 16, and finally another buy on November 8, 1985. This last buy was still in effect at this writing on May 9, 1986, during which time the Value Line Index had jumped some 20.7 percent.

Of these forty-two buys, only twenty were profitable, just 48 percent. However, these twenty profitable buys produced average profits of 15.3 percent per trade. The twenty-two losing trades, on the other hand, lost only 3.9 percent per trade. Cumulatively, the forty-two trades yielded an average net gain of 5.2 percent. Annualized, that 5.2 percent works out to 17.9 percent. When playing the market, I believe strongly in cutting your losses short and letting your profits run, and this is a perfect example of how this philosophy works in practice. It's an ideal strategy for the speculator . . . and not a bad idea for the traditional investor either.

On the sell side, results were similar. Had you sold short on the sell signals, you would have profited twenty-two times in forty-two trades for an average gain of 8.9 percent. In the twenty wrong instances, your average loss would have been only 3.6 percent. Overall, the average gain per short-side sale comes to 2.9 percent, which annualizes to 14.4 percent.

Totaling long and short sales, 50 percent were losers, but the average loss was only 3.8 percent. This compares with an average gain of 11.9 percent on the 50 percent that were profitable. With an average profit per trade of 4.1 percent, the annualized return from trading with the Four Percent Model netted 16.4 percent, far above the 2.0 percent return you would have achieved had you merely bought and held the Value Line Index.

There's no question about it—this very simple model

TABLE 27

SUMMARY OF FOUR PERCENT MODEL VS. VALUE LINE COMPOSITE INDEX MAY 6, 1986 TO APRIL 12, 1985

Type of Trade	Number of Trades	% Profit per Trade	Average Days per Trade	Annualized Profit
Buys (long)				
Losses	22 (52%)	− 3.9%		
Gains	20 (48%)	+ 15.3		
Net	42 (100%)	+ 5.2	94	+ 17.9%
Sells (short)				
Losses	20 (48%)	− 3.6		
Gains	22 (52%)	+ 8.9		
Net	42 (100%)	+ 2.9	70	+ 14.4%
Total				
Losses	42 (50%)	− 3.8		
Gains	42 (50%)	+ 11.9		
Net	84 (100%)	+ 4.1	82	+ 16.4%

$10,000 became $176,596 in 18.9 years
(+ 16.4% annualized return).
$10,000 buy-and-hold became $14,587
(+ 2.0% annualized return).

works well. Had you traded both the long and the short side since 1966, an initial $10,000 would have grown to $176,596, exclusive of dividends.

A virtue of this model is that you can use it as presented or alter it to your own preference. If you want fewer signals and fewer trades, you can increase the 4 percent rule to, say, 5 or 6 percent. This would probably give you a slightly lower return on a gross basis but save money on transaction costs. On the other hand, if you are more short-term-oriented, you might cut the rule to, say, 3 percent or even 2½ percent. You'd have more trades, probably a higher gross return, but greater transaction costs. To my mind, the 4 percent rule is a nice trade-off between excessive turnover on one hand and solid returns on the other.

Even better returns are provided when you combine the Four Percent Model with the Prime Rate Indicator. Together, they make a superior stock market timer, as we'll see in the following chapter.

CHAPTER 11

For the Model IRA Investor–
The Stock Market Timer

We're now ready to build what we will call the Stock Timer Model. The model is simplicity itself. It requires merely the two indicators we've developed in the last two chapters, the Prime Rate Indicator and the Four Percent Model. You will need only a few minutes a week to keep up with the two of them.

Table 28 shows the worksheet for the Stock Timer Model arbitrarily beginning on the last day of 1979. The left-hand column shows the date, and the next three columns enumerate three stock market averages, the Zweig Unweighted Price Index, the S&P 500, and the Dow Jones Industrial Average. The fifth column shows the condition of the Prime Rate Indicator. A "B" means that the indicator is on a buy signal; an "S" indicates that it is on a sell signal. The next column shows a similar grading for the Four Percent Model. The far-right column shows the rating for our overall Stock Timer Model.

To generate a buy signal on the Stock Timer Model, we must have *both* the Prime Rate Indicator and the Four Percent Model on buy signals. If either of those indicators is negative (on sell signals), then the Stock Timer Model will flip to a sell signal. This is the most conservative way to invest given these two indicators. They must be unanimously bullish, or we will withdraw from the stock market.

TABLE 28

STOCK TIMER MODEL WORKSHEET

Date	ZUPI	S&P 500	Dow	Prime Rate	Four Percent Model	Stock Timer Model
12/31/79	112.33	107.94	939	B	B	Buy
2/19/80	117.09	114.60	876	S	S	Sell
4/11/80	100.52	103.79	792	S	S	Sell
5/01/80	103.73	105.46	809	B	B	Buy
8/26/80	132.08	124.84	953	S	B	Sell
11/07/80	133.15	129.18	932	S	S	Sell
11/14/80	138.18	137.15	986	S	B	Sell
12/12/80	128.32	129.23	917	S	S	Sell
12/22/80	132.87	135.78	959	B	S	Sell
12/26/80	134.98	136.57	966	B	B	Buy
4/24/81	148.46	135.14	1020	S	B	Sell
6/16/81	149.84	132.15	1003	B	B	Buy
6/22/81	149.02	131.95	994	S	B	Sell
7/10/81	144.14	129.37	956	S	S	Sell
9/21/81	127.04	117.24	847	B	S	Sell
10/02/81	126.78	119.36	861	B	B	Buy
1/15/82	128.45	116.33	848	B	S	Sell
2/01/82	128.68	117.78	852	S	S	Sell
3/08/82	121.07	107.34	795	B	S	Sell
3/16/82	120.96	109.28	798	S	S	Sell
4/02/82	127.71	115.12	839	S	B	Sell
5/28/82	127.76	111.88	820	S	S	Sell
7/26/82	124.39	110.36	825	B	S	Sell
8/20/82	126.35	113.02	869	B	B	Buy
7/29/83	205.39	162.56	1199	B	S	Sell
8/10/83	200.53	161.54	1176	S	S	Sell
9/23/83	209.93	169.51	1256	S	B	Sell
10/21/83	204.43	165.95	1249	S	S	Sell
11/25/83	207.01	167.18	1277	S	B	Sell
2/03/84	201.64	160.91	1197	S	S	Sell
8/03/84	187.22	162.35	1202	S	B	Sell
10/15/84	194.61	165.77	1203	B	B	Buy
11/30/84	193.25	163.58	1189	B	S	Sell

(TABLE 28 continued)

STOCK TIMER MODEL WORKSHEET

Date	ZUPI	S&P 500	Dow	Prime Rate	Four Percent Model	Stock Timer Model
1/11/85	200.36	167.91	1218	B	B	Buy
5/03/85	214.71	180.08	1247	B	S	Sell
6/07/85	226.04	189.68	1316	B	B	Buy
8/16/85	227.71	186.11	1313	B	S	Sell
11/08/85	230.66	193.72	1404	B	B	Buy
5/09/86*	284.28	237.85	1789	B	B	Buy

*Last date of study.

Now refer to the first line on the worksheet. On December 31, 1979, our arbitrary starting date, both the Prime Rate Indicator and the Four Percent Model had been on buy signals dating back to December 7 (not seen on the worksheet). Therefore, the Stock Timer Model was on a buy signal. That buy endured until February 19, 1980, on which date both the Prime Rate Indicator and the Four Percent Model flipped to sell signals, generating a sell signal for the Stock Timer Model.

In managing the money, it is assumed that when the Stock Timer Model is on a buy signal, the money is invested in no-load equity mutual funds. When the Stock Timer Model flips to a sell signal, the money is switched to money market funds, generally in the same family of funds as the equity fund. So, as of the close of February 19, 1980, one would have switched from equity funds (stocks) into money market funds.

On April 11, 1980, the Four Percent Model turned positive, giving a buy. However, that was not enough to turn our Stock Timer Model bullish because the Prime Rate Indicator was still on a sell signal. A few weeks later, on May

1, 1980, the Prime Rate Indicator gave a buy signal. That made it unanimous and the Stock Timer Model went to the buy side.

Market conditions remained bullish for nearly four months until August 26, 1980, when the Prime Rate Indicator gave a sell signal. Even though the Four Percent Model was still positive at that time, our ultraconservative approach generated a sell signal on the Stock Timer Model. That was a signal to switch from stock funds into money market funds.

On November 7, 1980, the Four Percent Model gave a sell signal as tape action deteriorated. The indicators were unanimously on sells, but our overall model had been negative anyway for more than two months. There were a few other changes in individual indicators over the next few months, but they both did not get into bullish gear until December 26, 1980. That triggered another buy signal from the Stock Timer Model. That signal stayed in effect until April 24, 1981, when the Prime Rate Indicator gave way and our Stock Timer Model turned to the sell side.

You can follow the work table thereafter right up until the last date of this study, when we cut it off on May 9, 1986. On that date, by the way, both the Prime Rate Indicator and the Four Percent Model were still bullish, so our overall Stock Timer Model was still on the buy signal that had been given on November 8, 1985.

You can set up such a worksheet on your own if you wish, although with just two indicators to follow it may not be necessary. Just remember that you need *both* the Prime Rate and the Four Percent Model on buy signals in order to be in the stock market. If one or the other (or both) is bearish (on sell signals), you should switch into money market funds.

Occasionally, you will miss an up market by this very conservative system. However, you will be able to sleep at night and you will be playing the stock market only when the odds are greatly in your favor. Sometimes the odds may be slightly in favor of the stock market going up, but we would just as soon stick with risk-free money market returns during those spans.

Now let's check the results of our Stock Timer Model all the way back to 1965. Table 29 shows how the Stock Timer Model performed when trading against the very broad-based Zweig Unweighted Price Index (ZUPI), a pretty good measure of the performance of the average NYSE stock. Remember, the ZUPI moves almost in lockstep with the Value Line Index. Later, in Table 32, we'll test the Stock Timer Model against the blue-chip-dominated Standard & Poor's 500 Index.

The test begins on the date of the first buy signal in 1965, namely January 15 of that year. The left-hand column of Table 29 shows the date of the particular signal, and the second column shows the type of signal—either buy or sell—given by the Stock Timer Model. Column 3 shows the value of the ZUPI as of the date of the signal. Columns 4, 5, and 6 are applicable only to the buy signals. Column 4 shows the percent appreciation in the ZUPI on each of those signals.

For example, the first buy signal was given when the ZUPI stood at 103.18 on January 15, 1965. As seen in the second line of the table, a sell signal was given on June 11, 1965, when the ZUPI had climbed to 105.30. This means that the ZUPI had appreciated by 2.1 percent during that time, and that is the number that you see in the fourth column of the first line under percent appreciation on buys. Check the third line of the table to see the results on the second buy signal, the one of August 13, 1965, at 110.70 on the ZUPI. That one stayed in effect for some seven months until March 10, 1966, when, as seen in the fourth line of the table, the ZUPI was up to 125.43. That represented a 13.2 percent increase in the ZUPI on the second buy signal, as noted on line 3 of the fourth column.

The fifth column of Table 29 is labeled "Estimated Dividends on Buys." I have estimated the percentage return of-

TABLE 29

TOTAL RETURNS ON STOCK TIMER MODEL VS. ZWEIG UNWEIGHTED PRICE INDEX 1965–86

Date	Signal	ZUPI	Appreciation on Buys	Estimated Dividends on Buys	Total Return on Buys	Interest Earned in Sell Periods	$10,000 Growth
1/15/65	B	103.18	+ 2.1%	+ 0.8%	+ 2.9%	–	$ 10,290
6/11/65	S	105.30				+ 0.6%	10,352
8/13/85	B	110.70	+ 13.2	+ 1.2	+ 14.4		11,842
3/10/66	S	125.43				+ 4.3	12,352
1/26/67	B	121.28	+ 19.5	+ 2.1	+ 21.6		15,020
10/27/67	S	144.90				+ 0.8	15,140
12/29/67	B	148.24	– 5.5	+ 0.3	– 5.2		14,352
2/09/68	S	140.11				+ 0.8	14,467
4/05/68	B	140.32	+ 4.4	+ 0.1	+ 4.5		15,118
4/19/68	S	146.45				+ 2.3	15,466
9/25/68	B	164.98	+ 7.7	+ 0.4	+ 8.1		16,719
12/02/68	S	177.68				+ 12.6	18,825
9/21/70	B	101.86	0.0	+ 0.2	+ 0.2		18,863
10/23/70	S	101.89				+ 0.7	18,995
12/04/70	B	105.69	+ 19.4	+ 1.3	+ 20.7		22,927
5/26/71	S	126.24				+ 2.5	23,500
12/03/71	B	113.67	+ 10.1	+ 0.9	+ 11.0		26,085
5/05/72	S	125.18				+ 10.6	28,850
1/29/74	B	79.17	+ 2.2	+ 0.4	+ 2.6		29,500
3/22/74	S	80.95				+ 4.5	30,932
10/21/74	B	53.83	– 5.1	+ 0.4	– 4.7		29,479
11/22/74	S	51.08				+ 0.9	29,744
1/03/75	B	50.20	+ 42.2	+ 2.3	+ 44.5		42,980
7/25/75	S	71.37				+ 1.8	43,753
11/14/75	B	67.89	– 4.2	+ 0.1	– 4.1		41,960
12/05/75	S	65.03				+ 0.5	42,169
1/02/76	B	68.37	+ 19.6	+ 0.8	+ 20.4		50,772
4/09/76	S	87.00				+ 1.7	51,635
8/02/76	B	84.79	– 1.3	+ 0.1	– 1.2		51,015
8/20/76	S	83.69				+ 0.4	51,219

(TABLE 29 continued)

TOTAL RETURNS ON STOCK TIMER MODEL
VS. ZWEIG UNWEIGHTED PRICE INDEX
1965–86

Date	Signal	ZUPI	Appreciation on Buys	Estimated Dividends on Buys	Total Return on Buys	Interest Earned in Sell Periods	$10,000 Growth
9/24/76	B	86.79	− 3.3%	+ 0.1%	− 3.2%		$ 49,580
10/08/76	S	83.91				+ 0.6%	49,878
11/26/76	B	86.24	+ 5.2	+ 0.8	+ 6.0		52,871
4/08/77	S	90.75				+21.8	64,396
12/07/79	B	110.96	+ 5.5	+ 0.9	+ 6.4		68,518
2/19/80	S	117.09				+ 2.8	70,436
5/01/80	B	103.73	+27.3	+ 1.5	+28.8		90,722
8/26/80	S	132.08				+ 3.7	94,079
12/26/80	B	134.98	+10.0	+ 1.2	+11.2		104,615
4/24/81	S	148.46				+ 2.3	107,022
6/16/81	B	149.84	− 0.5	+ 0.1	− 0.4		106,594
6/22/81	S	149.02				+ 4.3	111,177
10/02/81	B	126.78	+ 1.3	+ 1.3	+ 2.6		114,068
1/15/82	S	128.45				+ 5.2	119,999
8/20/82	B	126.35	+62.6	+ 4.8	+67.4		200,879
7/29/83	S	205.39				+11.8	224,582
10/15/84	B	194.61	− 0.7	+ 0.5	− 0.2		224,133
11/30/84	S	193.25				+ 1.0	226,374
1/11/85	B	200.36	+ 7.2	+ 1.0	+ 8.2		244,937
5/03/85	S	214.71				+ 0.7	246,652
6/07/85	B	226.04	+ 0.7	+ 0.5	+ 1.2		249,612
8/16/85	S	227.71				+ 1.5	253,356
11/08/85	B	230.66	+23.2	+ 1.5	+24.7	–	315,935
5/09/86*	–	284.28	–	–	–	–	–

Total Stock Timer Model return: $315,935
Annualized return on Stock Timer Model: +17.6%
Buy-and-hold return (including dividends): $27,552
Annualized return on buy-and-hold: +8.0%

*Last date of study.

fered by dividends on the broad-based market during the period that the Stock Timer Model was on a buy signal. For example, the first buy signal stayed in effect for roughly five months, from January 15 to June 11 of 1965. During that time, I've estimated you would have earned about eight tenths of 1 percent in dividends on the broad market.

Please note that dividend returns on the broad-based market are significantly lower than the returns on the blue-chip-dominated Standard & Poor's 500, whose large corporations generally pay higher dividends than many of the smaller firms that are also included in the ZUPI, which actually covers all listed NYSE stocks. In the third line of Table 29, which covers the results of the buy signal of August 13, 1965, you'll see that the estimated dividend return was 1.2 percent for the seven months in which that particular buy signal was in effect.

Column 6 of Table 29 shows the total return on the buy signals. This is nothing more than the addition of the returns in columns 4 and 5. That is, I have added the appreciation to the dividend returns and have come up with the total return. For the first buy signal on the first line, the total return is 2.1 percent for appreciation, plus .8 percent for dividends, which equals a 2.9 percent total return. For the second buy signal on line 3, the total return is 14.4 percent, found by adding 13.2 percent appreciation to the 1.2 percent dividends.

Column 7 applies only to the sell signal periods. It represents the estimated interest earned on money market accounts during the time one was on a sell signal. Line 2 shows that our Stock Timer Model gave a sell signal on June 11, 1965. That signal was in force for two months until the buy signal of August 13, 1965. Column 7 of line 2 shows that you would have earned an estimated six tenths of 1 percent while investing in money market funds during that span. The second sell signal is shown on the fourth line, coming on March 10, 1966. That one stayed in effect for ten and a half months, until

January 26, 1967. Using rates of interest prevailing in those days, you would have earned approximately 4.3 percent on your money.

Finally, the far-right column of Table 29 shows what would have happened to a $10,000 initial investment if you had traded the market according to the signals given by our Stock Timer Model. It is assumed that you would have invested in no-load mutual funds whose volatility and portfolio structure were similar to that of our ZUPI. This probably could have been accomplished by purchasing two or three funds which specialize in secondary stocks. It's then assumed that you would have gone into typical money market funds which invest in certificates of deposit, Treasury bills, and the like during the sell signal periods.

Starting with $10,000, you would have made 2.9 percent on the first buy signal of January 15, 1965 (column 7 of line 1). This means that $10,000 would have appreciated by 2.9 percent, so on completion of the buy signal in June 1965, the $10,000 would have grown to $10,290, as seen in the far-right column of line 1. The sell signal in June of that year lasted for two months, during which time you would have earned six tenths of 1 percent in interest. Compounding that on top of the $10,290 leaves an ending value of $10,352 as of August 13, 1965. That value appears in the right-hand column on line 2.

Let's try one more. The total return on the August 13, 1965, buy signal was 14.4 percent. Compounding that against a value of $10,352 on the date of the buy signal results in a total portfolio value of $11,842 as of March 10, 1966. That sum is seen in the far-right column of line 3.

In all, there have been twenty-seven buy signals given by the Stock Market Timer since 1965, an average of about 1¼ per year in the twenty-one-plus years since then. Overall, including the effect of dividends, twenty of the twenty-seven signals, or 74 percent of them, produced profits, not a bad batting average. Moreover, some of the seven losers produced rather insignificant losses, including declines of 1.2 percent in August 1976, .4 in June 1981, and .2 in October 1984. The worst loss was 5.2 percent as a result of a December 29, 1967, buy signal. That's not bad for a worst case. In other words, your portfolio never would have been cremated with our very conservative approach.

By contrast, some of the buy signals produced exceptional profits. The greatest was 67.4 percent, beginning in August of 1982. Other particularly good profits were 21.6 percent in January 1967, 20.7 percent in December 1970, 44.5 percent in January 1975, 20.4 percent in January 1976, 28.8 percent in May 1980, and 24.7 percent on the buy signal given November 8, 1985, one which was still in effect as of the cutoff of this study on May 9, 1986.

Obviously, you would have made money on every one of the sell signals because you would have been in risk-free money market funds. In all, over a span of about 21.3 years, an original investment of $10,000 in this trading approach, using the Stock Timer Model, would have appreciated to a hefty $315,935. That's an average annual compounded return of a very big 17.6 percent. By contrast, had you bought the broad market on January 15, 1965, and held it continuously until May 9, 1986, your $10,000 investment would have grown to only $52,032, a compounded annualized return of 8.0 percent a year.

In other words, using our ultraconservative Stock Timer Model approach to trading stocks, you would have more than doubled the long-run returns of the stock market (+ 17.6 percent versus + 8.0 percent), and you would have done so while staying at risk in stocks for a cumulative total of only 7.8 years out of the total holding period of 21.3 years. That works out to an invested exposure of only about 37 percent of the entire time.

To put this into English, your return would have better

than doubled that of the market and you would have been at risk just over one third of the time. Or to put it still another way, you'd have taken one third of the risk of an average investor and more than doubled his total return. In my book, that ain't bad.

Table 30 shows the same exact test except it's applied to the Standard & Poor's 500 stock index, which is a measure of the performance of blue chip stocks, generally speaking. One could easily achieve the S&P returns by buying no-load mutual funds which are diversified among predominantly blue chip issues. The returns against the S&P aren't quite as good, but there is a reason for that. The S&P simply is not as volatile as the broader-based Zweig Unweighted Price Index. Therefore, any in-and-out strategy involving the S&P isn't going to produce as high a return. Nonetheless, the returns are still quite pleasing.

Nine of the buy signals on the S&P lost money while one broke even out of twenty-seven trips to the plate. That's still a five-eighths success rate. Moreover, none of the losses were devastating and some of them were particularly small, such as a .6 percent loss in August 1976, the .9 percent loss in October 1981, the .7 percent loss in October 1984, and the 1.2 percent loss in June 1985. The worst loss was 6.5 percent back in December 1967. By contrast, some of the returns were gratifying, such as the 28.9 percent profit in January 1975, the 20.2 percent gain in May 1980, the hefty 49.6 percent profit in August 1982, and the 24.8 percent gain from November 1985 to May 9, 1986.

Overall, a $10,000 investment trading the S&P 500 would have grown to an ending value of $126,360, a compounded annualized return of 12.6 percent. A long-run investor using the buy-and-hold approach would have seen his $10,000 climb to $64,122 in the span of 21.3 years. These figures, of course, include dividends. That works out to a buy-and-hold return of 9.1 percent a year, some 3½ percentage points a year worse

TABLE 30

TOTAL RETURNS ON STOCK TIMER MODEL VS. S&P 500 INDEX 1965–86

Date	Signal	S&P 500	Appreciation on Buys	Estimated Dividends on Buys	Total Return on Buys	Interest Earned in Sell Periods	$10,000 Growth
1/15/65	B	86.21	− 1.3%	+ 1.5%	+ 0.2%	−	$ 10,020
6/11/65	S	85.12				0.6%	10,080
8/13/85	B	86.77	+ 2.5	+ 1.7	+ 4.2		10,503
3/10/66	S	88.96				4.3	10,955
1/26/67	B	85.81	+10.7	+ 2.5	+13.2		12,401
10/27/67	S	94.96				0.8	12,500
12/29/67	B	96.47	− 6.9	+ 0.4	− 6.5		11,688
2/09/68	S	89.86				0.8	11,781
4/05/68	B	73.29	+ 2.7	+ 0.1	+ 2.8		12,111
4/19/68	S	95.85				2.3	12,390
9/25/68	B	102.36	+ 5.6	+ 0.5	+ 6.1		13,146
12/02/68	S	108.12				12.6	14,802
9/21/70	B	81.91	+ 2.3	+ 0.3	+ 2.6		15,187
10/23/70	S	83.77				0.7	15,293
12/04/70	B	89.46	+11.3	+ 1.7	+13.0		17,281
5/26/71	S	99.59				2.5	17,713
12/03/71	B	97.06	+ 9.9	+ 1.3	+11.2		19,697
5/05/72	S	106.63				10.6	21,785
1/29/74	B	96.01	+ 1.3	+ 0.6	+ 1.9		22,199
3/22/74	S	97.27				4.5	23,198
10/21/74	B	73.50	− 6.3	+ 0.4	− 5.9		21,829
11/22/74	S	68.90				0.9	22,026
1/03/75	B	70.71	+26.3	+ 2.6	+28.9		28,391
7/25/75	S	89.29				1.8	28,902
11/14/75	B	90.97	− 4.6	+ 0.2	− 4.4		27,630
12/05/75	S	86.82				0.5	27,769
1/02/76	B	90.80	+10.5	+ 1.0	+11.5		30,962
4/09/76	S	100.35				1.7	31,488
8/02/76	B	103.19	− 0.8	+ 0.2	− 0.6		31,299
8/20/76	S	102.37				0.4	31,425

(TABLE 30 continued)

TOTAL RETURNS ON STOCK TIMER MODEL VS. S&P 500 INDEX 1965–86

Date	Signal	S&P 500	Appreciation on Buys	Estimated Dividends on Buys	Total Return on Buys	Interest Earned in Sell Periods	$10,000 Growth
9/24/76	B	106.80	− 4.0	+ 0.2	− 3.8		30,230
10/08/76	S	102.56				0.6	30,413
11/26/76	B	103.15	− 4.7	+ 1.1	− 3.6		29,317
4/08/77	S	98.35				21.8	35,708
12/07/79	B	107.52	+ 6.6	+ 1.1	+ 7.7		38,458
2/19/80	S	114.60				2.8	39,534
5/01/80	B	105.46	+18.4	+ 1.8	+20.2		47,520
8/26/80	S	124.84				3.7	49,228
12/26/80	B	136.57	− 1.0	+ 1.5	+ 0.5		49,524
4/24/81	S	135.14				2.3	50,664
6/16/81	B	132.15	− 0.2	+ 0.2	0.0		50,664
6/22/81	S	131.95				4.3	52,842
10/02/81	B	119.36	− 2.5	+ 1.6	− 0.9		52,367
1/15/82	S	116.33				5.2	55,090
8/20/82	B	113.02	+43.8	+ 5.8	+49.6		82,414
7/29/83	S	162.56				11.8	92,139
10/15/84	B	165.77	− 1.3	+ 0.6	− 0.7		91,494
11/30/84	S	163.58				1.0	92,409
1/11/85	B	167.91	+ 7.2	+ 1.3	+ 8.5		100,264
5/03/85	S	180.08				0.7	100,965
6/07/85	B	189.08	− 1.9	+ 0.7	− 1.2		99,754
8/16/85	S	186.11				1.5	101,250
11/08/85	B	193.72	+22.8	+ 2.0	+24.8	–	126,360
5/09/86*	–	237.85	–	–	–	–	–

Total Stock Timer Model return: $126,360
Annualized return on Stock Timer Model: + 12.6%
Buy-and-hold return (including dividends): $27,590
Annualized return on buy-and-hold: + 9.1%

*Last date of study.

than our trading strategy. Overall, we would have beaten the S&P's total return by some 3½ percentage points a year, once again taking only a bit more than one third the total risk of the buy-and-hold investor. On a risk-adjusted basis that's excellent.

CHAPTER 12

To Cut Security Risks—
The IRA Bond Trading Model

We've already developed a model on trading stock mutual funds which I think is the optimal approach for the IRA investor. But many of you may not want to undertake the perceived risk of investing in stocks, or at least not with all your money. The best alternative to stocks is to invest your IRA in no-load bond mutual funds and then switch out of those funds into money market funds when bond market conditions are too risky. Thus, you can use the bond trading model in this chapter as an alternative to the stock trading model or as a supplement to it. You might want to put half your money into stock mutual funds and half into bond mutual funds and trade them according to the models.

I owe credit to my colleague Ned Davis and his associate Loren Flath for designing this model especially for this book according to my general requirements. We tried to keep the model as simple as possible while adhering to two of my key general principles, which apply to the stock market as well—namely, staying in gear with the tape and in gear with the Fed.

The immediate problem with testing anything in the bond market is finding a suitable index of bonds. The stock market has no such problem thanks to the existence of the Dow Jones Industrial Average, the S&P 500 Index, and many more stock market indexes. It's very difficult to find a daily bond market index that goes back far enough to be of use. The best available is what's known as the Dow Jones 20 Bond Index, a composite of twenty corporate bonds.

Until 1977 this was called the Dow Jones 40 Bond Index because it had forty corporate bonds in it. We began this test in 1965 using the old Dow Jones 40 Bonds and then switched over to the Dow Jones 20 Bond Index in 1977. The Dow Jones 20 Bonds did not necessarily move in line with government bonds, but then that's always a problem because corporate bonds and government bonds can move out of step to a small degree, as you have already seen in the annual returns of bonds and stocks in Table 21 in Chapter 7.

The Dow Jones 20 Bond Index has a long history and is very easily available to the casual investor. The price updates on the Dow Jones 20 Bonds are found daily in the *Wall Street Journal* and on Quotron machines. Weekly summaries, which are probably adequate for your use, are printed in *Barron's*, a Dow Jones publication.

THE INDICATORS

Don't Fight the Tape

As you've already seen in discussing stocks, I find it crucial to always stay in gear with the tape or the trend of the tape itself. This applies equally to bonds. The model we're constructing to trade bonds consists of four indicators, two of which are trend-following or tape indicators. Both of these indicators monitor the weekly close of the Dow Jones 20 Bond Index itself. You needn't bother with any daily prices in this model. All you need is the weekly closing price as found in *Barron's*.

Tape Indicator A shown in Table 31 generates a buy signal when the Dow Jones 20 Bonds rises by six tenths of a

TABLE 31

TAPE INDICATOR A

Week Number	Dow Jones 20 Bond Average	
1	100.00	Low
2	100.60	Tape Indicator A gives "buy"
3	102.00	
4	102.50	
5	102.30	
6	103.00	
7	103.80	
8	104.20	
9	104.60	
10	105.00	Peak
11	104.70	
12	104.00	Tape Indicator A gives "sell"
13	103.00	

percent or more on a weekly close basis. Conversely, it generates a sell signal when the weekly close declines by six tenths of a percent or more from a prior peak. Let's try an example, as shown in Table 31.

Suppose the Dow Jones 20 Bond average is selling exactly at 100 and that it had been falling, during which time it was on a sell signal. Suppose that the lowest weekly close was 100.00. It would take a rise of six tenths of a percent, to a price of 100.60, in order to generate a buy signal. Suppose in week number one the index was 100.00 and then the index rallied in week two to 100.60. That would trigger the buy signal for Tape Indicator A.

Let's suppose over the following weeks the bond market continued a general rally with no weekly decline amounting to as much as six tenths of a percent. Suppose the Dow bonds hit 105 in week ten after having rallied for several weeks and then in week eleven closed at 104.70. That would be a down week but not enough to give a sell signal, which would require a drop to 104.37. Then suppose in week twelve the bonds fell to 104.00, or .37 below the trigger point. A sell signal would have been given in week twelve. That's all there is to it.

Remember, it takes a six tenths of a percent rise from any low weekly close in the bonds to give a buy signal and a six tenths of a percent decline from any weekly high in the bond prices in order to give a sell signal. The six tenths of a percent move need not take place in one week. It could take several weeks in order to give a signal.

Tape Indicator B, shown in Table 32, uses the same Dow Jones 20 Bonds but is less sensitive than Tape Indicator A. This second trend-following measure requires a 1.8 percent increase in the Dow 20 Bonds in order to give a buy signal and a 1.8 percent decline in the Dow 20 Bonds in order to give a sell signal. Again, all prices are calculated on a weekly basis. Let's try an example with the same bond averages, as shown in Table 32.

Suppose that in week one the bonds had been trending downward and were already on a sell signal and closed at 100.00. Let's also suppose that the bonds began to rally, rising to 100.60 in week two. That would not be enough to flip the B indicator bullish because that would not be a 1.8 percent increase from the 100.00 level. What would be needed is a weekly close of 101.80 or higher to give the buy signal.

Suppose in week three the Dow Jones 20 Bonds closed at 102.00. That would give the buy signal, since that is .20 above the 101.80 mark needed for the buy. Now you're on the buy signal at the end of week three. Suppose the bonds rally up to 105 in week ten. In week eleven, following the prior example, the bonds dropped to 104.70. Is that enough to give

TABLE 32

TAPE INDICATOR B

Week Number	Dow Jones 20 Bond Average	
1	100.00	Low
2	100.60	
3	102.00	Tape Indicator B gives "buy"
4	102.50	
5	102.30	
6	103.00	
7	103.80	
8	104.20	
9	104.60	
10	105.00	Peak
11	104.70	
12	104.00	
13	103.00	Tape Indicator B gives "sell"

a B sell? No. A 1.8 percent decline from 105.00 would require a level of 103.11 or less.

Just use your trusty calculator or use pencil and paper to factor out the 1.8 percent decline. In week twelve the bonds dropped to 104. That's still not enough to give the sell signal. Suppose in week thirteen the bonds then fall to 103. Would that give a sell? Yes. Remember, 103.11 is a 1.8 percent drop from 105, and therefore the 103 level is .11 below that necessary to give a sell. Thus, week thirteen would generate a sell signal on Tape Indicator B.

So both tape indicators (combined in Table 33) use the same underlying index, the Dow 20 Bonds, in order to view the trend. The difference is that Tape Indicator A is more sensitive, requiring only a .6 percent movement on a weekly

TABLE 33

TAPE INDICATORS A AND B

Week Number	Dow Jones 20 Bond Average	
1	100.00	Low
2	100.60	Tape Indicator A gives "buy"
3	102.00	Tape Indicator B gives "buy"
4	102.50	
5	102.30	
6	103.00	
7	103.80	
8	104.20	
9	104.60	
10	105.00	Peak
11	104.70	
12	104.00	Tape Indicator A gives "sell"
13	103.00	Tape Indicator B gives "sell"

change basis in order to give signals, while Tape Indicator B requires a 1.8 percent change from a prior peak or trough to give the same type of signal.

It would be too cumbersome to list all of the signals generated by these two trend-following methods. However, I will summarize them for you. From January 1, 1965, to when this study was completed on March 14, 1986, Tape Indicator A, the more sensitive of the two, gave 114 signals in just over twenty-one years. Sixty-eight of them, or 60 percent of the total, were profitable. Had you purchased the Dow Jones 20 Bonds on each buy signal and sold the Dow 20 Bonds and moved into Treasury bills during sell signal periods, you would have made 12.1 percent per year. On the other hand, had you bought and held the Dow Jones 20 Bonds for the 21¼-year period under study, you would have made only 5.9 percent a year.

Of course, I'm assuming no transaction costs, which is unrealistic. But nor am I advocating that you make 114 trades in a twenty-one-year period. That would be too many. However, this indicator adds quite a bit to our model, as we'll see later.

Tape Indicator B, the less sensitive one, gave only forty-eight signals over the 21¼ years, of which thirty, or 63 percent, were profitable. However, the annualized return following this method was only 9.2 percent a year versus 5.9 percent for buy-and-hold. We cut down the number of trades significantly by using the 1.8 percent "filter" as opposed to the .6 percent "filter." However, we reduced our annualized return. This often happens when you test tape-following indicators. If you make them very, very sensitive, you'll generate huge numbers of trades which theoretically lead to great returns. But, of course, after transaction costs in the real world, the actual returns wouldn't be nearly as high.

By slowing down our trend-following method and generating fewer transactions, we cut down the theoretical rate of return but we also lowered the actual transaction costs. The optimal sensitivity for our indicator is reached by a trade-off between transaction costs and theoretical return.

That may sound like a mouthful, but all you need to know now is that the trend-following indicators work and they add a tremendous amount to our overall model. There are other significant components, as we will see in a moment.

Don't Fight the Fed

We have now developed two trend-following indicators. It is also important to have an indicator which follows the action of the Federal Reserve itself. Ironically, this particular Fed indicator produces a return a tad below that of the buy-and-hold return for our test period. However, it's still important to stay in gear with the actions of the Federal Reserve. If you fight the Fed long enough, you're bound to get into trouble.

If I were trading bonds myself, I would perhaps use a more complicated bond indicator. But here I'm trying to keep everything as simple as possible. We will use only the change in the discount rate for this Fed indicator on the bond market. The discount rate is that rate the Fed charges banks who wish to borrow from the Fed. When the Fed changes the discount rate, which generally happens only a few times a year, it is very widely reported in the newspapers and even on the network news.

A buy signal is generated when the discount rate is cut by a half percentage point or more. The sell signal is given when the discount rate is raised half a point or more by the Fed. That's all there is to it.

If perchance the discount rate had been falling and the Fed increased it by only a quarter point, it would not give a sell signal. It would take a full half-point increase to give a sell. Of course, two separate quarter-point increases in the discount rate would suffice to give a sell signal, and two quarter-point cuts would generate a buy signal.

In Table 34 I've given you a hypothetical example of how changes in the discount rate would produce various signals on the indicator. In case 2 the discount rate rose ½ percent, giving a sell signal. That stayed in effect until case 7, when the discount rate was lowered ½ percent, tripping a buy signal. In case 10 the discount rate rose ¼ percent to 8.75, but that is not enough to give a sell signal. But in case 11 it rose still another ¼ percent to 9.00. The total of the two increases was ½ percent, sufficient for a sell signal. Finally, in case 14 the discount rate was sliced a full percent, giving a buy signal.

TABLE 34

DISCOUNT RATE INDICATOR

	Discount Rate	Point Change	Rating
1.	8.00%		
2.	8.50	+ ½	Sell
3.	9.00	+ ½	Sell
4.	9.50	+ ½	Sell
5.	9.75	+ ¼	Sell
6.	10.00	+ ¼	Sell
7.	9.50	− ½	Buy
8.	9.00	− ½	Buy
9.	8.50	− ½	Buy
10.	8.75	+ ¼	Buy*
11.	9.00	+ ¼	Sell*
12.	9.50	+ ½	Sell
13.	10.00	+ ½	Sell
14.	9.00	− 1	Buy

*Combined, these two ¼-point rises totaled ½ point for sell signal.

Such Fed following has given only ten signals in the 21¼-year test period, of which six were profitable. But the results of trading the model—that is, buying the Dow Jones 20 Bonds on the buy signals and switching into T-bills on the sell signals—generated an annualized return of only 5.7 percent, just a hair below the buy-and-hold return of 5.9 percent. Again, however, you are much better off staying in gear with the Federal Reserve when playing the bond market. Moreover, though this individual indicator is not suitable for use entirely on its own, it adds quite a bit when used in conjunction with the other three indicators in our bond model.

Changes in the discount rate don't occur very often, and when they do they always make the front page of the business section and almost as often the front page of any major newspaper. You can also review *Barron's* over the weekend to make doubly sure if there was a change in the discount rate by the Fed. It's very easy to get these data.

The Yield Curve

The Yield Curve Indicator is a more indirect way to measure what the Federal Reserve is doing. Think of it as another Fed indicator if you wish. If the Fed decides to tighten up and create a so-called money crunch—usually to cool off an overheated economy—the Fed will drive up short-term interest rates to the extent that they will exceed long-term interest rates. This is called an *inverted yield curve*, which is the opposite of the normal condition when long-term rates, representing bonds, which are riskier, exceed the return on short-term rates such as T-bills, which are less risky.

An inverted yield curve, therefore, is a sign of a "tight" Fed and is generally a bearish condition for stocks and bonds. A "normal" yield curve—one in which long-term rates are above short-term rates—is generally favorable for stock and bond prices.

Specifically, our Yield Curve Indicator uses *Moody's AAA corporate bond rate* on a weekly average basis for the long-term interest rates and *90-day commercial paper rates* as a short-term interest rate. The difference between the two is what we are measuring here. The data on Moody's AAA corporate bonds can be obtained directly from Moody's with a subscription to one of their weekly publications (Moody's Survey, 99 Church St., New York, NY 10007; 212-553-0300). Alternatively, you can get the numbers weekly in a publication produced by the St. Louis Federal Reserve Bank. That publication, which is free of charge, is called *U.S. Financial Data* (Federal Reserve Bank of St. Louis, P.O. Box 442, St. Louis, MO 63166). The commercial paper rate is also available in that publication and in *Barron's* statistical section.

To calculate the yield spread, simply subtract the commercial paper rate from the AAA bond rate. For example, if bond rates are 10 percent and commercial paper rates are 8 percent, the yield spread would be +2.00 percent. If, say, AAA rates were 12 percent and commercial paper rates were 13 percent, the yield spread would be −1.00 percent. A buy signal on the Yield Curve Indicator develops when the yield curve is +.60 percent or greater. In other words, it is bullish when long-term rates are .60 percent or more above short-term rates. A sell signal develops when the Yield Curve Indicator equals −.20 percent or less. Thus, it is bearish when short-term rates go above long-term rates by at least .20 percent.

The Yield Curve Indicator also has a neutral zone. We will consider its condition neutral when the yield curve is anywhere between +.60 and −.20. Anything above that range is considered bullish and would count as +1 in the model which we will develop. Anything below that range is considered bearish and will be graded −1 in our model. Anything in the neutral zone will be considered as zero points for our model. Table 35 gives a brief example of how to grade the Yield Curve Indicator.

As seen in week one, the yield curve is −1.00, giving it a negative (bearish) reading of −1 point. Over the next few weeks the yield curve narrows, finally reaching −.10 in week four. That pushes the rating up a notch to a neutral zero. Thereafter the yield curve continues to improve, finally hitting +.70 in week seven. That's above our bullish zone of +.60, so our rating jumps to a positive +1. The yield curve peaks at +1.20 in week nine, and finally declines to +.50 in week eleven. Since that's below the +.60 bullish cutoff, the rating slips to a neutral zero.

Testing the Yield Curve Indicator, it gave thirteen signals in the 21¼-year period beginning in 1965, of which nine, or 69 percent, were profitable. Trading the Dow Jones

TABLE 35

SAMPLE YIELD CURVE INDICATOR

Week Number	Moody's AAA Corp. Bonds	Commercial Paper	Yield Curve	Rating on Yield Curve Indicator*
1	10.00%	11.00%	−1.00%	−1
2	10.00	10.50	−0.50	−1
3	9.80	10.10	−0.30	−1
4	9.70	9.80	−0.10	0
5	9.60	9.40	+0.20	0
6	9.50	9.10	+0.40	0
7	9.50	8.80	+0.70	+1
8	9.20	8.20	+1.00	+1
9	9.40	8.20	+1.20	+1
10	9.30	8.50	+0.80	+1
11	9.40	8.90	+0.50	0
12	9.40	9.00	+0.40	0

*+1 = Buy signal
0 = Neutral
−1 = Sell signal

20 Bonds, it returned 8.0 percent per annum versus 5.9 percent for buy-and-hold. That may not seem like much, but it does make an important contribution to the bond-timing model we are about to build.

CONSTRUCTING THE BOND MODEL

I've just described how to give points to the Yield Curve Indicator. Remember a buy signal is worth +1 in the model, which is any yield curve of +.60 percent or higher. A sell signal is worth −1 point in our signal, which is any yield curve of −.20 percent or less. Any yield curve between those ranges is graded a neutral zero. The other three indicators in our model are even simpler. Buy signals are worth +1 point, and sell signals are worth −1 point. That is true for both of the Dow 20 Bonds trend-following indicators and the Fed indicator. Thus, our bond trading model can range from a high of +4 points down to a low of −4 points.

The model gives a buy signal when it reaches +3 points or greater and remains on the buy until the model falls to −3 points or worse. Once a sell signal is triggered, our bond trading model remains on that sell until the model again reaches +3 points or greater in order to render another buy signal.

Table 36 shows a sample Bond Model worksheet. In week one all four indicators in the Bond Model are positive and the model itself is at +4 points, for a buy signal. After

TABLE 36

SAMPLE BOND MODEL WORKSHEET

Week	TAPE INDICATORS A	B	Discount Rate	Yield Curve	Total	Rating
1	1	1	1	1	4	Buy
2	−1	1	1	1	2	
3	−1	−1	1	1	0	
4	−1	−1	1	0	−1	
5	−1	−1	1	0	−1	
6	−1	−1	−1	0	−3	Sell
7	−1	−1	−1	−1	−4	
8	−1	−1	−1	−1	−4	
9	+1	−1	−1	−1	−2	
10	+1	+1	−1	−1	0	
11	+1	+1	+1	0	3	Buy
12	+1	+1	+1	+1	4	

that, various indicators begin to lose ground. By week six the rating dips to −3 points, just enough to trip a sell signal for the Bond Model. Eventually, some indicators recover and by week eleven the rating has worked its way up to +3 points. That's sufficient for a buy signal.

Table 37 shows the results of our Bond Timer Model since January 1965. It is assumed that when the model gave a buy signal (+3 points or more), you would have bought the Dow Jones 20 Bond Index, and when the model gave a sell signal (−3 points or lower), you would have sold the Dow Jones 20 Bonds and switched into 90-day U.S. Treasury bills. No allowance has been made for transaction costs. In reality, though, you would not be buying the Dow Jones 20 Bond Index, but rather a *no-load bond mutual fund*, and on sell signals you would be switching into a money market fund, probably part of the same family of mutual funds. For that, there would be *no* transaction charges, assuming that you were dealing with no-load funds . . . the types of funds I recommend for this switching strategy.

The reason we ran this test backward against the Dow Jones 20 Bonds is that there were no or few no-load bond mutual funds available over the entire period, and there were no money funds whatsoever prior to the early 1970s. I feel that this test, however, is a fair approximation of what you could have or would have done over the past twenty-one-odd years had such no-load bond funds and money market funds been in existence since 1965.

When you buy bonds, you receive not only the capital gains or losses on the changes in bond prices but also the interest payments. Thus, in this test, when one is "long" with the bonds, we've included the interest earned as well as the capital gain or loss. For example, if bond prices over a year rose from 100 to 105 and interest of 10 percent was paid, the ending "total return bond index" for that year would be 115, representing the total return on bonds. Such a total return

TABLE 37

RESULTS OF BOND MODEL TRADING
1965 TO 1986

Signal	Date	Bond Price*	Profit on T-bills	Profit on Bonds†	Days Held	$10,000 Growth
Sell	1/08/65	–	+ 9.4%	–	735	$10,936
Buy	1/13/67	104.43		+ 0.3%	126	10,968
Sell	5/19/67	104.73	+ 2.9		238	11,289
Buy	1/12/68	100.96		– 0.2	35	11,268
Sell	2/16/68	100.77	+ 2.3		154	11,527
Buy	7/19/68	102.53		+ 1.5	63	11,695
Sell	9/20/68	104.02	+14.2		735	13,356
Buy	9/25/70	98.25		+28.4	889	17,146
Sell	3/02/73	126.14	+ 7.1		336	18,359
Buy	2/01/74	130.29		+ 0.1	35	18,372
Sell	3/08/74	130.38	+ 7.0		308	19,648
Buy	1/10/75	126.16		+41.1	1015	27,728
Sell	10/21/77	178.04	+ 5.3		294	29,202
Buy	8/11/78	181.69		+ 0.8	49	29,434
Sell	9/29/78	183.13	+18.6		595	34,920
Buy	5/16/80	169.02		– 4.7	133	33,279
Sell	9/26/80	161.08	+16.4		385	38,746
Buy	10/16/81	152.00		+ 1.6	119	39,346
Sell	2/12/82	154.35	+ 0.5		14	39,553
Buy	2/26/82	159.72		+ 5.4	119	41,681
Sell	6/25/82	168.32	+ 0.5		14	41,887
Buy	7/09/82	169.17		+35.9	637	56,942
Sell	4/06/84	229.98	+ 1.9		70	58,027
Buy	6/15/84	226.68	–	+58.1	637	91,690
–	3/14/86‡	358.19	–	–	–	–

*Price for bonds *includes* interest accumulated beginning Jan. 8, 1965.
†Profit on bonds *includes* interest earned.
‡Last date of study; no sell signal.

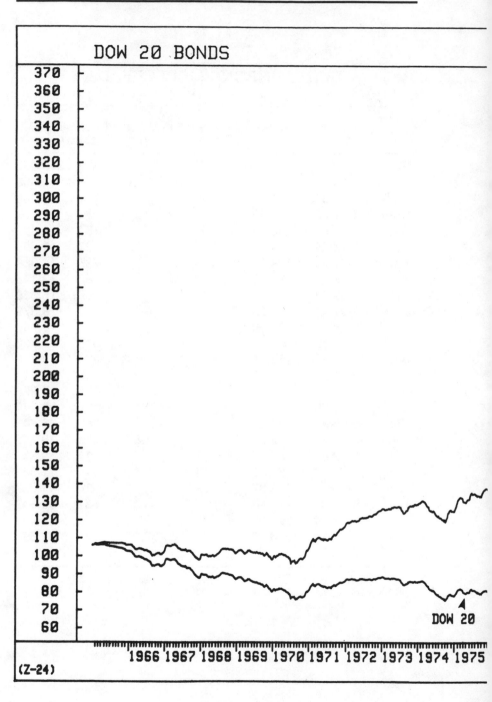

DOW 20 BONDS

(Z-24)

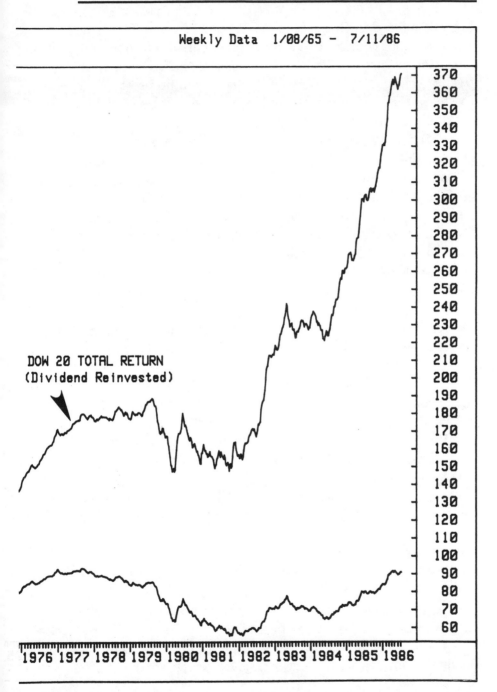

Weekly Data   1/08/65 -   7/11/86

DOW 20 TOTAL RETURN
(Dividend Reinvested)

index is plotted in Graph E on the Dow 20 Bonds. The same bonds without considering interest payments are also plotted in the lower part of Graph E. You'll notice that over the past twenty years or so the Dow 20 Bonds wound up pretty close to where they began, after having fallen for years and then making a U-turn upward in 1981.

However, the Dow 20 Bonds Total Return Index ended at about 360, up from 100 in 1966, thanks to twenty-one years of continuous interest payments (although after the ravages of inflation, that produced only a tiny "real" profit). Even interest payments could not eliminate all of the damage during the vicious bond bear market from 1979 to 1981, although they did take out some of the sting.

Table 37 shows that our Bond Timer Model gave twenty-three signals since 1965. Twenty-one of them, or 91 percent, generated profits. Obviously, all of the sell signals would have been profitable, since we would have gone into risk-free Treasury bills on them. Of the twelve buy signals, ten were profitable on a total return basis—that is, including interest earned. The first unprofitable signal was in early 1968, when you would have been in bonds for only about five weeks and would have lost two tenths of a percent. The only significant loss came in mid-1980 when you would have held bonds for 4½ months and lost 4.7 percent. That's not bad for the worst loss in over twenty-one years.

By contrast, some of the bond holding periods were handsomely profitable, including a 2½-year stretch beginning in September 1970 which netted 28.4 percent; a 2¾-year period beginning in early 1975 which showed a 41.1 percent profit; a 1¾-year period starting in July 1982 which produced a 35.9 percent gain; and the still open trade (as this is written) that began in June 1984 and has gone 1¾ years to date, showing a 58.1 percent profit, the best of the bunch.

A $10,000 initial investment in trading the Dow 20 Bonds according to our model would have become worth $91,690 in just under 21¼ years. That's an annualized rate of 11.0 percent. By contrast, had you bought the Dow 20 Bonds at the beginning of 1965 and held them, you would have made only 5.9 percent per annum. All of that gain and more on buy-and-hold was accounted for by interest income alone. The bond prices themselves actually declined moderately over the twenty-one years, as seen in the lower portion of Graph E.

The graph begins a year after our test period in early 1966, but there was only moderate downward change in the prices during 1965. From a price of a little over 100 in early 1966 the bonds skidded into the mid-50s at the bear market low in 1981. As I write this, the Dow Jones 20 Bonds are a little bit over 90. In other words, you would have lost roughly 10 percent of your money in price depreciation by holding long-term bonds over the 21¼ years, roughly half a percent a year. But you would have made close to 6.5 percent a year in interest, for a net return of about 5.9 percent a year.

Graph F shows how our bond timing signals looked against the Dow 20 Bonds Total Return Index. Each "S" with a down arrow shows the sell signals, the same ones listed in Table 37. The "B's" with up arrows are the buy signals, whose exact dates also appear in Table 37.

The top portion of Graph G shows the dollar results of our Bond Timer Model. In other words, starting with $100 (or an Index of 100), the ending value would have risen to almost $500 from bond trading alone. The lower portion is the Dow 20 Bond Total Return Index (the same as that plotted on the top part of Graph E).

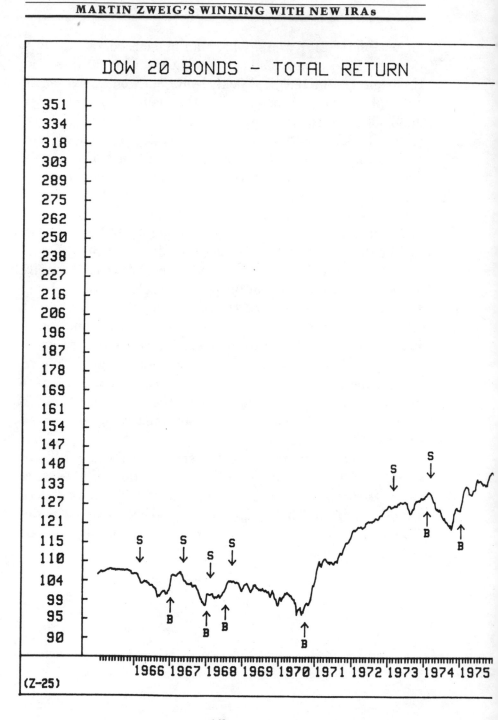

DOW 20 BONDS – TOTAL RETURN

(Z–25)

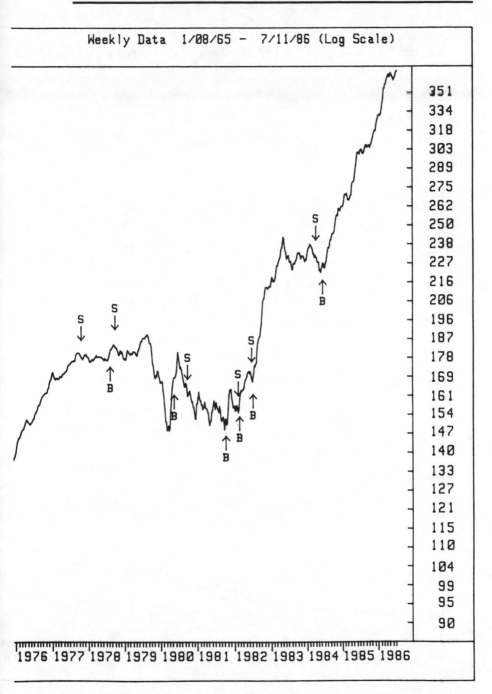

Weekly Data   1/08/65 -   7/11/86 (Log Scale)

Effect of Trading Dow 20 Bonds (Includes

Scale is in $$ and Reflects
Initial $1,000 Investment

Switch to T Bills on Sell Signals
(Returns are Compounded)

9000
8500
8000
7500
7000
6500
6000
5500
5000
4500
4000
3500
3000
2500
2000
1500
1000

1967 1968 1969 1970 1971 1972 1973 1974 1975 19

Dividends)

Weekly Data 3/04/66 - 7/11/86

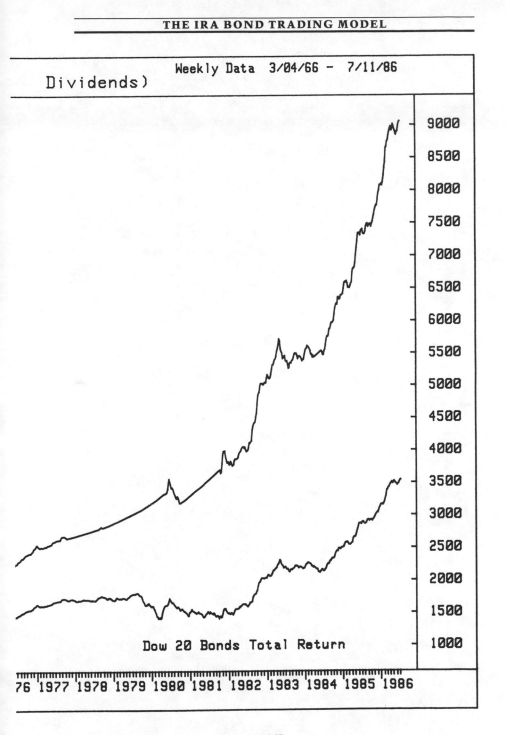

Dow 20 Bonds Total Return

76 1977 1978 1979 1980 1981 1982 1983 1984 1985 1986

CHAPTER 13

Questions and Answers About IRAs

Is there any way I can realistically project my retirement needs?

The further away from retirement you are, the harder it is to know how much money you'll need to achieve your desired life-style. Your present age, current income, economic prospects, and family status must be considered. As a rule of thumb, you'll probably do pretty well if your retirement income equals about 75 to 80 percent of your working income. A lower amount could spell troublesome times ahead.

In calculating your income needs at retirement, many factors are involved. For one thing, certain of your work-related expenses such as commutation, restaurant lunches, and appropriate dress clothing will be reduced. In addition, if you're living in your own home, the mortgage might be paid off, saving a significant chunk of money.

When totaling pros and cons of retirement costs, you must consider that your medical expenses could be higher, against which you might want to protect yourself with additional insurance to supplement Medicare. On the other hand, you might decide that you have sufficient capital and drop some of your life insurance.

There are many financial variables depending on your individual scenario for retirement. For example, would you want to budget heavy expenses for travel, recreation, hobbies, or whatever else you have been looking forward to doing after the nine-to-five routine ends? Will you want to relocate to another part of the country? Will you want to provide financial assistance to children and grandchildren?

Another financial factor to consider when you stop working is that you probably will want to discontinue setting aside money for your retirement years. There will be less incentive to save—this is the time you have been waiting for to put your retirement funds to work for you. Moreover, your income taxes presumably will be lower because of decreased earnings, which is where the beauty of your IRA account comes in. All the money you withdraw probably will be taxed at a much lower rate than you would have paid at your time of peak earnings.

Perhaps hardest to predict will be the extent to which inflation distorts your income status at retirement. With the economic future so nebulous, your best bet is to maximize your present savings and select the IRA investment program that best fits your current income and projected retirement goals.

In this book you describe so many different types of mutual funds—income funds, growth and income funds, government bond funds, special-interest funds, and so on. How can I know which is best for my IRA?

The main factor is your own risk preference. If you're very conservative and can't afford to lose much money, then a growth fund or an aggressive growth fund is not for you. Even a fund that invests in long-term bonds or in blue chip common stocks might be a bit risky. It depends upon just how much money you feel you can afford to lose. Of course, in an IRA plan, you probably aren't going to be needing the money for quite a few years down the road.

But as you approach your expected retirement age—say, sixty-five, and you are now sixty-two—then the amount of risk you can afford to accept becomes smaller and smaller. If you lose money at this stage, you don't have much time left to recoup it. Moreover, you're going to *need* that money to live on, so there is no point in gambling. To put it another way, I would "never gamble with the rent money."

Now, I've also tried to show in this book that most people can afford to accept the risk of a stock mutual fund—even an aggressive one—or a long-term bond fund if they get out of the market when the risk is very high. It's the bear markets in stocks and bonds which create the bulk of the damage. If you can eliminate most of those periods—even if you have to give up some of the bull market gains along the way—you can afford to play the stock or bond markets without exposing yourself to undue risk.

If, though, you feel that you still don't want to use my timing models or that it's too much effort on your part to work with them, and if you still don't want to take on much risk, then about all that's left open to you are short-term money market instruments such as certificates of deposit or money market funds which invest in them. Unless you are rapidly approaching retirement age, however, I don't think they are the most appropriate vehicles. But if you are that risk-averse, maybe you'd want them.

Are all discount brokers the same? How do I choose one?

No. Not all discount brokers are the same. I don't deal with any of them directly myself, so I doubt that I could tell you which ones are better than others. But at least as a starter, I would suggest dealing with the larger ones of national stature that have good reputations such as Fidelity, Quick & Reilly, and Charles Schwab. That does not necessarily exclude others.

You want to make sure that they all have adequate insurance, and I would prefer dealing only with those that are members of the New York Stock Exchange. After that, it's really a question of judging the service that you get. Even within a single brokerage firm, one customer might get relatively good service and another relatively poor service depending on exactly whom they are dealing with. On average, though, from what I've heard through the grapevine, the large discount brokers seem to do a pretty good job.

Some money managers have advertised to manage your stock IRAs. Generally speaking, is this a good investment idea?

Presumably you mean going to a money manager who will manage your IRA individually—that is, not lumped together in a mutual fund. If you are talking about an account as small as $2,000, the economics are not very good for the money manager. That means he's likely to charge a fee which is relatively high in proportion to your assets, unless he's managing this account for you as a favor because you have a much larger account in some other form with him.

I would also question how much diversification you would get holding an individual account. The least that I would do is find out what the fees are, what the diversification is, and how your account will be managed relative to the other accounts at that particular money manager. If the management fee is something like 5 percent a year or so, I would pass.

You really have to ask yourself, What can an individual manager do in segregating my $2,000 or $5,000 account that I cannot get in a well-diversified mutual fund? If you are talking about an IRA that is considerably larger, perhaps because the funds have been rolled over into an IRA, then an individual money manager might make sense. That bracket usually begins at somewhere around $50,000 or higher.

How large an impact are IRAs having on the movement of the overall stock market now?

There's definitely been a net inflow of cash into the stock market because of IRAs. They are so new that very few people have liquidated stock-invested IRAs, and a lot of new money has been coming in. So each year since the current IRA regulations went into effect about five years ago, the positive cash inflow has helped stock prices go higher. The net annual inflow now is probably several billion dollars into the stock market. That sounds like a lot, but it's still a relatively small number given the trillion-dollar-plus size of the stock market.

Nonetheless, the IRAs have had a positive impact and even more so in the first part of the year when the bulk of IRA money traditionally comes in. Most people seem to wait till after the first of the year to fund their IRAs and stop investing after April 15. So the bulk of the money comes in between January and mid-April.

I'm also thinking about the IRA money that goes into stock mutual funds as well as IRA money that is invested in stocks directly. Both have been having a positive impact and both will continue to have a positive impact for quite a number of years. This positive cash flow will eventually slow as retirees begin to withdraw money in significant sums from their IRAs. However, that day is many years away.

By the way, as I mentioned in the first chapter, the possible impact on the stock market might be extremely large as more and more people shift away from CDs and money market funds and into stocks. Potentially, the impact could be even greater than the moderately positive boost that I've discussed here.

What about limited partnerships? Do they make sense for IRAs?

Almost always the answer is no. Most, but not all, limited partnerships are for investments in real estate, oil, agriculture, and other areas where certain tax benefits such as depreciation or amortization accrue to the investor. This is irrelevant in an IRA, where your taxes are deferred anyhow. There's no economic advantage investing in tax shelters here.

Now, there are a few limited partnerships that invest in more conventional assets such as stocks and bonds and which offer no particular tax advantages. Indeed, I run such a venture myself. The catch here, though, is that the more aggressive investing generally done in these limited partnerships is probably not suitable for IRAs. Moreover, the amount required in such limited partnerships usually far exceeds the $2,000 or so that you might kick in for your IRA.

Very few limited partnerships will open an account for less than $50,000 to $100,000 minimum, and even then there are personal wealth and income requirements of a relatively high nature which would preclude many investors from such ventures. So, in general, the answer is that limited partnerships for IRAs don't make sense.

I've been reading about TIGRs from Merrill Lynch, CATS™ from Salomon Brothers, Treasury receipts (TRs), Stripped Treasuries from PaineWebber. Are these all the same? What are their advantages and disadvantages for IRAs?

They are all fairly similar, although there are some modifications from firms that sponsor these vehicles. TIGRs or CATS™ in general are what's known as zero coupon Treasury bonds. Let's take an example. Suppose you could buy a U.S. Treasury bond with a twenty-year maturity that carries a 10 percent coupon on it. In other words, you would receive 10 percent of the face value of the bond as an interest payment each year for twenty years and then you would receive the $1,000 principal repayment from the government twenty years out.

What the brokerage firms have done here is to strip away the interest payment for the investor. They take that interest payment and repackage it into another security for sale. What's left is simply a promise by the U.S. Government to pay you $1,000 twenty years later, but without any interest payments. Obviously, such a security would be nowhere near worth $1,000 today because somebody else is going to wind up getting the interest on that bond, not you. You get zero in interest. Hence the term "zero coupon."

Nonetheless, such a zero coupon security has value because you are going to receive $1,000 in twenty years. The question is: What price should that security sell today to equate it with the going interest rate? If you use an interest rate of 10 percent, the zero coupon bond (or TIGR) would sell for roughly $150 today. That's on the assumption that if you could compound $150 at 10 percent a year, it would grow into $1,000 over twenty years. Or put it this way: If you gave the government $150 today in return for $1,000 to be paid by Uncle Sam twenty years down the road (no interest payments being given), it would be the equivalent of receiving 10 percent a year on your money.

Why would an investor want to buy a zero coupon bond when he can purchase a regular bond that pays interest? The answer is that interest rates can fluctuate and cause reinvestment problems for the investor. Suppose you could buy a regular twenty-year bond today with a 10 percent coupon. Suppose interest rates fall to 5 or 6 percent in a year or two. Your bond would go up in price quite a bit from the original starting price, but eventually it's going to sink back down to $1,000 when it's paid off at maturity in twenty years.

You have received $100 in interest payments in year one and you now have to reinvest that money. But when you turn around, you find that bonds are yielding only 6 percent. So the money would be reinvested at a lower rate than that which prevailed when you first bought the bond. If such a trend were to continue throughout the bulk of the twenty-year holding period, you would find that your final return would be less than 10 percent because each time you'd reinvest you'd be reinvesting at a lower rate. Of course interest rates could go up and you would actually make a bit more money by reinvesting at higher rates, although presumably rates would rise only if inflation rose, and your real return might not be so high.

So zero coupon bonds offer the investor a way of "locking in" a given rate of return on bonds for a very long period. The reinvestment problem is eliminated. However, two additional problems accrue. The first is that because there is no interest payment made, the price of the bond is extremely volatile. If interest rates rise moderately, the bond price will fall significantly. If bond prices rise dramatically, the price of the bond could be crunched.

That might not make too much of a difference to you in an IRA, where you're not going to want the money for twenty years. Nonetheless, it can give you headaches and there is an opportunity cost involved—that is, why pay $150 for a zero coupon bond today when the price might be down to $100 a year from now?

The second problem is that Uncle Sam makes you pay income tax on the assumed interest earned each year, even though it is not actually paid on a zero coupon bond. For example, you buy the zero coupon bond at $150 and receive $1,000 for it twenty years out. The entire $850 gain is considered interest payments by Uncle Sam and is spread out over the life of the bond and taxed accordingly, even though you have no net cash inflow. Therefore, TIGRs and other zero coupon bond vehicles generally make no sense at all for a tax-paying investor.

In an IRA, of course, you don't have that problem. Taxes on the "phantom interest" are deferred until you begin taking the money out for retirement. So you need not pay income tax on phantom income during the holding period of the zero coupon bond. This is why zero coupons in the form of CATS®, TIGRs, and other vehicles have become very popular in IRAs. But popular or not, zero coupon bonds are extremely volatile and are not suitable for a risk-averse investor. Only those people willing to take on the extreme volatility should invest in zero coupon bonds.

Should I ever consider gold and precious metals funds for my IRA?

I don't see any reason why not, provided that you have a way of dealing with the major trend in the prices of gold and/or silver. The vehicle could be gold and silver stocks if your account is large enough to justify the commissions for buying individual stocks, or a suitable mutual fund with diversified portfolios in such investments. I would generally not put all of my IRA money into a precious metals fund, but a portion of it would be reasonable.

You might elect a very long-term investment by placing 10 percent of your IRA in a gold mutual fund. This would give you some protection against inflation that could be especially valuable if a large chunk of your remaining IRA holdings were in, say, bonds. Alternatively, you might develop some model for gold and silver—perhaps somewhat similar to the overall stock timing model I presented in this book—with which you could time the gold funds.

But gold and silver, like any other investments, can go down in price at times. There have been and will be, from time to time, large bear markets in precious metals and it's neither fun nor profitable riding through them. So, just as with regular stocks, there's a time to be in precious metals and a time not to be.

Are there any advantages to insurance company annuities for IRAs?

The advantage is that you are locking in a known amount of value at the time you retire. This eliminates the downside and also the uncertainty about how much money you will have at retirement age. The disadvantage is that you don't know what inflation is going to run between now and your retirement period.

Suppose you buy an annuity that works out to a compounded rate of 10 percent. Say inflation heats up to 12 percent over the twenty-year period from now until your own retirement. You would come out a loser in real dollars of 2 percent a year. Or suppose inflation runs even 7 percent a year; you would make only 3 percent per annum in real dollars, which is not exactly terrific. I hate to guess what the inflation rate will be. By moving in and out of stocks and bonds you can deal with inflation a lot better. By locking yourself into an annuity you've lost a lot of control.

However, you could protect yourself to some extent by not putting all of your money into an annuity. Suppose you put 80 to 90 percent into an annuity and put the remaining 10 to 20 percent into a precious metals fund. That would presumably give you some protection against inflation.

What about a financial planner to help me meet retirement goals? Do I need one? Where do I find one?

An IRA is only one part of your overall financial needs and you really should be thinking about your total picture. I guess it wouldn't hurt to go to a financial planner. I'm not exactly sure how you go about finding them. Some are affiliated with brokerage firms, but I'd be a little cautious going there because they might be partial to in-house products.

There are independent planners around and they do have trade associations: the Institute of Certified Financial Planners, Denver, Colorado; the International Association for Financial Planning, Atlanta, Georgia; and the National Association of Personal Financial Planners, Arlington Heights, Illinois. I would certainly check out any planner's fees and qualifications with the trade associations. If you feel they are up to snuff, listen to what each has to say.

I would, however, be leery of any particular investment they try to sell you. If they tell you to buy a mutual fund or a stock or a bond and you buy it through a different channel, then there is no conflict of interest. If they try to sell you something in-house, ask them what kind of fee or commission they are going to be getting on that. They might not be totally objective in that case and what you want is objectivity. I would lean toward a financial planner who is not selling his or her own product.

Since my IRAs are so important to my future security, should I stick to the most conservative investments?

Well, I certainly wouldn't want to shoot craps. Stocks have a pretty good advantage over most other financial assets in that, in the long run, they tend to produce a higher return than bonds or cash. Bonds, while providing a lower long-run return than stocks, do provide a higher return than cash equivalents. The problem, as I've noted before, is that both stocks and bonds are volatile and they can go down at times—even the blue chip stocks and bonds. So stocks and bonds have risks.

177

You can cope with the risk in one of two ways. One is to avoid investing in them or perhaps only investing part of your money. You avoid the risk that way but you also lose out on the potentially higher returns. The second method is to invest in stocks and/or bonds but sell them during periods of high risk. You are not always going to be right with your timing, but if you can avoid the worst of a bear market and capture good pieces of a bull market, you'll wind up earning the long-run return available in stocks, probably even a greater return than the buy-and-hold investor would get, *and* you've chopped your risk down considerably.

Many of my friends have purchased Ginnie Mae mutual funds for their IRAs. Is this a good idea?

Ginnie Maes aren't much different from long-term bonds. If interest rates rise, the prices of Ginnie Maes fall. That's the risk that you have to take investing in these vehicles. I've already shown numerous times that the risk in stocks and bonds can be considerable during bear periods. So if you are going to buy Ginnie Maes, I would suggest that you follow the bond timing model seen in Chapter 12 and use it to sell these funds when conditions become very risky. When the model is bullish, investments in Ginnie Maes, regular bonds, or zero coupon bonds would be reasonable.

In view of current market conditions, aren't government se-curity funds returning 8 to 10 percent a better place for cash than money market funds at 5.5 to 6 percent?

Any investment with a yield considerably above money market rates automatically entails risk. In this case I pre-sume that you mean a pool of longer-term government securities. Again, you're getting into something more the equivalent of the bond market, not the money markets. So if you're going to do it, again, go back to the bond timing model in Chapter 12.

Are there any circumstances when a self-directed IRA brokerage account would be advantageous?

Yes, there are such circumstances. First, you should have enough money in the IRA account to get adequate diversification. Your initial $2,000 won't do it. Second, it should be at either a discount broker or at a full-service firm that will at least give you a break on the commission. If you've got $10,000 in your account and you're going to put only $2,000 into any one stock, the normal commission at a full-service broker would be high. You'd have to be able to negotiate it down somewhat to make it worth your while.

Given that you have enough money for the diversification and reasonable commissions, the only thing left is the willingness to pick stocks on your own. A lot of people prefer to do that. I would generally advise, though, that you should have $20,000 or $25,000 in such an account before beginning to pick stocks. Otherwise, I would put the money into a mutual fund.

There is, however, a type of mutual fund that you can buy through a self-directed IRA at a brokerage firm. This is called a closed-end investment fund or closed-end investment trust. There are more than 60 such funds around, some concentrating in stocks, some buying only bonds. The bigger ones are traded on the NYSE; others trade on the AMEX and the rest OTC. The Zweig Fund, for example, with $300 million in assets, is traded on the NYSE (symbol ZF).

All are mutual funds which trade in the market. But when you want to buy their shares, you don't buy them directly from the fund; you buy them in the marketplace just as you would buy any other stock. When you sell a closed-end fund, you don't redeem it back to the fund itself, but rather you sell it in the open market, again, just like a stock.

You could buy only one or two such funds and get the diversification, which might not be a bad idea. You would be paying a brokerage commission on your purchase, but it's a heck of a lot less than the "full-load" commission that you would pay to buy a full-load mutual fund. Of course, the brokerage commission is higher than the zero load or zero commission that you would pay on a no-load fund.

Is it to my advantage to stick to a single IRA vehicle or should I shop around each year for the best investment?

I think it is valuable to shop around. Conditions in the securities markets change and there is no point in sticking with a particular stock or fund or bond if the environment becomes hostile for that particular instrument. Clearly, as I've pointed out in the book, if you buy stocks or stock mutual funds, there's a time to shift out of them into money market funds. That means in effect that you are shopping around for a better vehicle, given certain conditions. The same would apply in switching between bond funds and money funds as explained in Chapter 12.

You might go one step further and stick with stock funds when our stock model is positive. When the stock model turns negative, but the bond model is still positive, you might switch into bonds. When both stock and bond models are negative, go into the money funds.

I would limit investments, however, to one of those three areas: stocks, bonds, and money market funds. Ginnie Maes would fall in the category of bonds; CDs would be in the area of money market funds. I would avoid real estate investments with an IRA, and insurance annuities are really more in the area of bonds.

Some advertisements claim that IRAs can make me a millionaire. Is this really true? How much must I invest, over how long a period of time, to make $1 million?

Yes, it is possible to reach the million-dollar asset value in an IRA. What you need is plenty of time and a very healthy rate of return. If you keep contributing $2,000 a year, for example, you would reach the $1 million net asset mark in thirty years if you were to earn a 15 percent annualized rate, which is a rather high return although certainly not impossible. Our stock timing model has done better than that in the past. By increasing the return to 17 percent, your $2,000 a year contribution would hit the million-dollar mark in twenty-eight years.

Stretching the return to 20 percent, you'd get there in twenty-five years. If you could earn 25 percent—which I would think is unreasonably high—you could hit the million-dollar figure in twenty-one years. At the nearly impossible rate of 30 percent, your contributions would accrue into $1 million within nineteen years.

If your investment returns are more modest, it simply just takes a long time to hit the million-dollar mark. For example, at 12 percent a year it takes thirty-six years, at 10 percent a year forty-one years. If you are curious about which combinations of years and returns wind up with various ending values, please consult Tables 2 to 5 in Chapter 2.

In your book Winning on Wall Street *you stress the importance of diversification. Does this principle also apply to my IRAs?*

Yes, it does as far as the stock market is concerned. That's why if you have less than $20,000 or so in your IRA, I advise you to buy one or possibly two different diversified mutual funds. In doing so, you will have more diversification.

If you buy stocks directly, you should buy at least five or six of them to get adequate diversification, but it gets awfully expensive attempting that with very small amounts of money, say, $2,000 or $5,000. That's why you should have $20,000 or more before you really start buying stocks individually.

In the bond market, diversification is not as important, especially if you are buying government securities, since government securities tend to move together to a great degree. But if you are going to buy corporate bonds individually, rather than in a mutual fund, I would spread the risk by buying bonds in different industries and/or different companies. Diversification up to a point is always a virtue.

Does it ever make sense to make an early withdrawal from my IRA before I reach age fifty-nine and a half?

Normally, you wouldn't want to withdraw the money early because you'd have to pay a penalty of 10 percent of what you take out, plus the normal income tax rate on anything withdrawn. However, if you absolutely must have the money, then just go ahead and pay the penalty and do it. Of course, an alternative might be to borrow money in the short run to cover your financial needs rather than touch your IRA.

The real question here is, Should you actually go ahead and invest in an IRA long before retirement if you expect that you might have to withdraw the money early at some future date and pay the 10 percent penalty? The answer depends on how many years you are going to keep your IRA before you withdraw any money and what rate of return you will earn in the interim.

For example, if you've had the IRA for only a year and earned less than 10 percent on your money, you would be worse off if you withdrew the funds. The longer you hold the IRA and the greater the rate of return, the better off you are even if you have to pay the penalty later. You're also better off the higher the tax bracket you're in, because the IRA will defer more taxes over that span.

Let's try an example. Suppose that you're forty years old, and you set up an IRA today, funding it each year with $2,000. Assume that you're in the 35 percent tax bracket and that your IRA earns 12 percent a year, which is consistent or even conservative for the models which we have presented in this book on stocks and bonds. At the end of ten years, when you're age fifty, your IRA will have $39,309 in it and you will have put up $20,000 of that yourself. The rest will have been profits on your investments.

Suppose, when you're at age fifty, your son or daughter is off to college and you decide to withdraw $40,000 to pay for that ghastly tuition expense. *Ugh!* In this example we'll use the round number of $40,000 and assume that you did just a tad better than 12 percent, because I want to keep it as a round number. How would you have faired over this period by having invested in the IRA?

First, on your $40,000 withdrawal you would pay a $4,000 penalty to the government, leaving you with $36,000. You would also pay income tax on 35 percent of the remainder. You would be left with $23,400 after the withdrawal, hopefully enough to get junior through one semester. Please bear in mind, though, that eventually you are going to have to pay income tax on the money you withdrew anyhow. Of course, that comes in your retirement years, and if your other income is down, your tax bracket might be lower.

In any event, you do have $23,400 free and clear after ten years and after paying penalties and income tax. Now suppose you had never opened an IRA; how would you have fared? First of all, the $2,000 you salted away each year would have been only $1,300 after you paid income tax at the 35 percent bracket in years one through ten. Remember, each year you were putting $2,000 into your IRA account you were not paying any income tax against it. Had you tried to keep the money, you would have had to give 35 percent of it away to Uncle Sam each year. So your accumulation would have been only $1,300 a year in an investment vehicle.

Now suppose that you could have invested $1,300 in a mutual fund or whatever and traded with one of our models and earned a gross return of 12 percent a year. To simplify it, let's say that the average tax rate on your 12 percent earnings was 33 percent, leaving you an effective after-tax rate of only 8 percent to have been compounded over the ten years. In other words, your alternative to the IRA would have been $1,300 (after taxes) each year for ten years to be compounded at an 8 percent after-tax rate (not a 12 percent rate). At year ten you would have $20,340 in your investment account. There would be no tax obligation on this because you would have paid your taxes all the way along.

However, that's still $3,060 less than what you would have accumulated in the IRA because of the tax advantages you would have received in the IRA even though it meant paying a 10 percent penalty in year ten. In other words, even if after ten years you had to withdraw the money and pay an early 10 percent penalty, you would come out significantly ahead of what you would have achieved without an IRA.

Again, I must stress that the longer you hold the IRA, the greater the annual return you can earn on your investments; and the higher your tax bracket, the better off you are going into an IRA, even if you eventually have to pay a penalty for early withdrawal.

What happens to my IRA in case of divorce?

IRAs are increasingly included in divorce financial settlements. Pursuant to a divorce decree or written agreement pertaining to the separation, an IRA or part of an IRA can be shifted from one spouse to another. It is important to note that the transfer of IRA funds is not considered a distribution by IRS and consequently no tax consequences result from this transaction.

For example, if a husband's IRA is transferred to his wife as part of a settlement, he has no tax obligations on this amount even if he is under fifty-nine and a half. From the effective date of the transfer, the IRA is treated as though it had been originally established by the wife. However, if she fails to roll over the money into an IRA within the deadline period, she is liable for the taxes on the assets received.

Note: All taxable alimony and court-ordered separate maintenance payments can be considered suitable "compensation" for contributing to an IRA. Since these rules are complex and subject to court interpretations and legislative changes, it would be prudent to get professional counsel in this area before making any decisions.

Can I use my IRA as security for a loan?

No. Under IRA regulations, you are not permitted to borrow from your IRA or to use it as collateral for a loan to another party. Should you make such a loan, it would be considered a distribution subject to the 10 percent withdrawal penalty, as well as taxable income for you in the year the transaction occurred.

Do I pay any taxes when I switch my IRA investments?

No. If you make the transfers according to IRA regulations (not taking personal possession of the assets or, if you do, redepositing them in another IRA within sixty days), these transactions are not considered distributions and are not subject to tax. All taxes are deferred until you start making withdrawals.

185

What happens if, after I reach age seventy and a half, I neglect to withdraw the minimum required amounts from my IRA?

Beware. Should that happen, you'll be hit by the stiffest penalty the IRS imposes on improper IRA distributions—a 50 percent tax on the amount that should have been withdrawn but was not.

Let's say you had $500,000 in your IRA and should have withdrawn approximately $40,000 in your first year but took out only $20,000. You would be socked with a $10,000 penalty tax (50 percent of the remaining $20,000 that should have been withdrawn). Since the rules on mandatory distribution rates are so important and so subject to confusion, I strongly advise that you carefully check with your IRA custodians and your accountant before you begin withdrawals after age seventy and a half.

Can I include foreign-earned income in determining the amount of my IRA contribution?

No. Foreign earned income is not considered "compensation" for making deductible contributions to an IRA. Only earned income on which you would normally pay federal income tax qualifies for IRA contributions. In calculating your gross income for the year for IRA purposes, you must reduce your compensation by the amount of your foreign-earned income exclusion and foreign-housing exclusion.

It would be convenient if I could automatically transfer funds from my checking account to my IRA. Is this permissible?

No problem there. Since various financial institutions might have different regulations, consult your bank and IRA trustee about the specific procedure to follow.

If I withdraw money from my IRA after reaching age fifty-nine and a half, can I also make contributions until I reach seventy and a half?

Yes. Of course any amounts you withdraw from your IRA after age fifty-nine and a half are subject to tax as ordinary income and you pay no penalty. If your earned compensation makes you eligible for additional IRA contributions in any year between ages fifty-nine and a half and seventy and a half, you may continue to make contributions and take advantage of the accompanying tax deferrals.

Aside from my income tax reports, is there any other verification to IRS about the status of my IRAs?

You bet there is. IRA trustees and custodians must file annual reports to IRS on the status of each IRA account they carry on their books, including any interest or dividend income earned as well as any penalties imposed. Your reported figures are matched by IRS computers with those from your IRA trustees, and you will be informed if there are any discrepancies.

I overlooked the IRA deadline last year and failed to make a contribution. Can I double up this year?

Sorry. IRS regulations are very specific in spelling out that you cannot make up in subsequent years any amounts you failed to contribute in any single year. However, if you skip a year or contribute less than the $2,000 maximum in any year, it has no bearing on your eligibility to contribute up to $2,000 in any future year in which you have sufficient earned income.

I have a self-directed IRA at my broker which includes stocks and bonds. Are any losses in these securities tax-deductible?

They are not. Remember, you already have taken a tax deduction on the amounts contributed to your IRA and, as far as IRS is concerned, you can only go that route once.

Are there any IRA investments that I should avoid?

Since all earnings of your IRA are already tax-sheltered, it would be counterproductive to build your portfolio with tax-free municipal bonds and tax-free money funds. These generally pay below-market interest rates because of their tax-sheltered status. You are therefore better off with non-sheltered investments, which usually generate higher income. All your earnings—regardless of source—are taxed as ordinary income when withdrawn from an IRA.

What transactions are prohibited for IRAs? Are there any penalties for such transactions?

The IRS defines a "prohibited transaction" as any improper use of your IRA or annuity. Examples of prohibited transactions with an IRA include borrowing money from it, selling property to it, and receiving unreasonable compensation for managing it.

Penalties for such transactions are severe. Generally, if you engage in a prohibited transaction in connection with your IRA during the year, it will not be treated as an IRA as of the first of the year. Once this happens, you must include the fair market value of part or all of the IRA assets in your gross income for the year. The fair market value is defined as "the price at which the IRA assets would change hands between a willing buyer and a willing seller, when neither has any need to buy or sell, and both have reasonable knowledge of the relevant facts." You must use the fair market value of the assets as of the first day of the year in which you engaged in the prohibited transactions. You may also have to pay the 10 percent tax on premature distributions.

Other prohibited transactions and their penalties:

Pledging an account as security: If you use part of your IRA as security for a loan, that part is treated as a distribution and is included in your gross income. You may also have to pay the 10 percent tax on premature distributions.

Borrowing on an annuity contract: If you borrow money against your IRA annuity contract, you must include in your gross income the fair market value of the annuity contract as of the first day of your tax year. You may also have to pay the 10 percent premature distribution tax.

Investment in collectibles: If your IRA invests in collectibles including works of art, rugs, antiques, metals, gems, stamps, coins (except gold or silver coins issued by the U.S. Government), alcoholic beverages, and other tangible personal property, the amount invested is considered distributed to you in the year invested. This means that the tax advantages of IRAs have been effectively eliminated for this kind of investment. The 10 percent tax on premature distribution may also apply.

Directory of Mutual Funds (as of August 28, 1986)

*U*nless otherwise specified, all funds listed on pages 192–95 accept IRAs and Keoghs and have no sales load or redemption fees. Minimum initial investments are often waived or reduced for IRA, Keogh, and pension accounts. Funds that do not have managed programs for those plans will open accounts for "self-directed" plans.

PAST PERFORMANCE

Mutual Funds	One-Year Profit Projection	Risk Rating	Correction 7/4/86– 8/22/86	1986 12/31/85– 8/22/86	12 Months 8/23/85– 8/22/86	Telephone	State	Minimum Initial Investment ($)
AARP CAP. GRTH	+ 17%	LOW	− 4%	+ 18%	+ 28%	800-253-2277	MA	250
AARP GRTH & INCOME	+ 22%	VERY LOW	0%	+ 19%	+ 35%	800-253-2277	MA	250
AFUTURE	+ 5%	VERY HIGH	− 10%	+ 8%	+ 16%	800-523-7594	PA	500
AMA—GRTH	+ 16%	HIGH	− 5%	+ 17%	+ 29%	800-523-0864	PA	300
AMA—MED. TECH.		HIGH	− 7%	+ 28%	+ 49%	800-523-0864	PA	500
AMERICAN INVESTORS	+ 4%	VERY HIGH	− 6%	+ 8%	+ 19%	800-243-5353	CO	400
ANALYTICAL OPT. EQUITY	+ 6%	MEDIUM	+ 1%	− 15%	− 10%	714-833-0294	CA	25,000
ARMSTRONG ASSOC.	+ 6%	VERY HIGH	− 1%	+ 12%	+ 20%	214-744-5558	TX	250
AXE-HOUGHTON B	+ 19%	VERY LOW	0%	+ 22%	+ 38%	800-431-1030	NY	1,000
AXE-HOUGHTON STOCK	+ 17%	VERY HIGH	− 4%	+ 17%	+ 35%	800-431-1030	NY	1,000
BABSON ENTERPRISE	+ 20%	LOW	− 6%	+ 11%	+ 17%	800-422-2766	MO	1,000
BABSON GRTH	+ 17%	MEDIUM	0%	+ 21%	+ 39%	800-422-2766	MO	500
BANCROFT CONVERT.	+ 18%	MEDIUM	+ 3%	+ 24%	+ 39%	CLOSED- END AMEX		
BARTLETT BAS. VALUE	+ 13%	VERY LOW	− 3%	+ 14%	+ 25%	800-543-8721	OH	1,000
BEACON HILL MUTUAL	+ 16%	MEDIUM	− 7%	+ 11%	+ 30%	617-482-0795	MA	0
BERGER—100	+ 12%	HIGH	− 8%	+ 28%	+ 42%	303-837-1020	CO	250
BERGER—101	+ 22%	VERY LOW	− 2%	+ 20%	+ 35%	303-837-1020	CO	250
BOSTON CO. CAP. APPR.	+ 21%	MEDIUM	0%	+ 23%	+ 40%	800-343-6324	MA	1,000
BOSTON CO. SPEC. GRTH	+ 10%	HIGH	− 9%	+ 15%	+ 27%	800-343-6324	MA	1,000
BRUCE	+ 24%	MEDIUM	− 2%	+ 38%	+ 67%	312-236-9160	IL	1,000
BULL & BEAR CAP. GRTH	+ 14%	HIGH	− 8%	+ 11%	+ 24%	800-431-6060	NY	1,000
BULL & BEAR EQUITY INCOME	+ 17%	VERY LOW	+ 1%	+ 20%	+ 33%	800-431-6060	NY	1,000
CALVERT EQUITY	+ 11%	HIGH	− 2%	+ 16%	+ 31%	800-368-2748	MD	2,000
CALVERT SOC. MGD. GRTH	+ 16%	VERY LOW	− 2%	+ 21%	+ 32%	800-368-2748	MD	1,000
CASTLE CONVERT.	+ 15%	HIGH	+ 3%	+ 18%	+ 13%	CLOSED- END AMEX		
CENTRAL SECURITIES	+ 19%	HIGH	+ 1%	+ 9%	+ 18%	CLOSED- END AMEX		
CENTURY SHARES	+ 26%	MEDIUM	− 2%	+ 21%	+ 40%	800-321-1928	MA	500
COLUMBIA GRTH	+ 18%	HIGH	− 6%	+ 13%	+ 27%	800-547-1037	OR	1,000
DIVIDEND GRTH DIV'D	+ 13%	LOW	− 2%	+ 12%	+ 15%	800-638-2042	MD	300
DIVIDEND GRTH LASER	− 10%	VERY HIGH	− 14%	− 13%	− 7%	800-638-2042	MD	300
DODGE & COX BALANCED	+ 17%	VERY LOW	− 2%	+ 15%	+ 31%	415-981-1710	CA	250
DODGE & COX STOCK	+ 21%	MEDIUM	− 2%	+ 15%	+ 35%	415-981-1710	CA	250
DREYFUS CONVERT. SECS.	+ 19%	VERY LOW	0%	+ 21%	+ 34%	800-645-6561	NY	2,500
DREYFUS FUND	+ 16%	LOW	0%	+ 17%	+ 27%	800-645-6561	NY	2,500
DREYFUS GWTH OPPTY.	+ 15%	LOW	− 2%	+ 15%	+ 31%	800-645-6561	NY	2,500
DREYFUS THIRD CENTURY	+ 13%	LOW	− 2%	+ 6%	+ 15%	800-645-6561	NY	2,500
EVERGREEN	+ 22%	LOW	− 4%	+ 22%	+ 36%	800-635-0003	NY	2,000
EVERGREEN TOT. RET.	+ 24%	VERY LOW	+ 5%	+ 26%	+ 40%	800-635-0003	NY	2,000
FEDER. STK. BD. (BANKS)	+ 17%	VERY LOW	+ 2%	+ 8%	+ 18%	800-245-5000	PA	25,000
FEDER. STK. TR. (BANKS)	+ 24%	LOW	+ 1%	+ 20%	+ 35%	800-245-5000	PA	25,000
FIDELITY CONTRAFUND	+ 13%	HIGH	− 2%	+ 11%	+ 27%	800-544-6666	MA	1,000
FIDELITY FREEDOM	+ 21%	HIGH	− 3%	+ 18%	+ 37%	800-544-6666	MA	1,000
FIDELITY FUND	+ 18%	MEDIUM	− 2%	+ 19%	+ 33%	800-544-6666	MA	1,000
FIDELITY GRTH & INCOME			− 2%	NA	NA	800-544-6666	MA	2,500
FIDELITY PURITAN	+ 20%	VERY LOW	+ 1%	+ 17%	+ 25%	800-544-6666	MA	1,000
FIDELITY QUAL. DIV'D (CORP)	+ 27%	VERY LOW	+ 8%	+ 27%	+ 38%	800-544-6666	MA	50,000

PAST PERFORMANCE

Mutual Funds	One-Year Profit Projection	Risk Rating	Correction 7/4/86– 8/22/86	1986 12/31/85– 8/22/86	12 Months 8/23/85– 8/22/86	Telephone	State	Minimum Initial Investment ($)
FIDELITY TREND	+18%	MEDIUM	− 5%	+17%	+31%	800-544-6666	MA	1,000
FIDELITY VALUE	+10%	HIGH	− 1%	+21%	+32%	800-544-6666	MA	1,000
FIDUCIARY CAP. GWTH	+11%	HIGH	− 8%	+14%	+24%	414-271-6666	WI	1,000
FINANCIAL DYNAMICS	+10%	VERY HIGH	− 8%	+12%	+22%	800-525-8085	CO	1,000
FINANCIAL PROG. IND.	+15%	HIGH	− 4%	+12%	+29%	800-525-8085	CO	1,000
FINANCIAL PROG. IND. INC.	+21%	LOW	− 2%	+19%	+36%	800-525-8085	CO	1,000
FLEX-FUND RETR. GWTH	+14%	LOW	− 2%	+21%	+32%	800-325-3539	OH	2,500
FOUNDERS EQUITY INCOME	+16%	VERY LOW	+ 5%	+16%	+22%	800-525-2440	CO	1,000
FOUNDERS GRTH	+18%	MEDIUM	− 2%	+29%	+44%	800-525-2440	CO	1,000
FOUNDERS MUTUAL	+21%	HIGH	− 2%	+24%	+47%	800-525-2440	CO	1,000
FOUNDERS SPECIAL	+17%	MEDIUM	− 3%	+26%	+31%	800-525-2440	CO	1,000
GATEWAY OPTION	+11%	VERY LOW	− 1%	+10%	+16%	800-354-6339	OH	500
GENERAL SECS.	+16%	LOW	0%	+11%	+33%	612-332-1212	MN	100
GINTEL ERISA	+19%	LOW	0%	+18%	+33%	800-243-5808	CT	2,000
GINTEL FUND	+15%	MEDIUM	0%	+18%	+25%	800-243-5808	CT	2,000
GRADISON EMERG. GWTH	+20%	MEDIUM	− 2%	+25%	+42%	513-579-5700	OH	1,000
GRADISON ESTAB. GWTH	+19%	MEDIUM	+ 3%	+15%	+28%	800-543-1818	OH	1,000
GROWTH INDUS. SHARES	+14%	HIGH	− 6%	+15%	+25%	312-346-4830	IL	200
HARTWELL GRTH	+17%	VERY HIGH	+ 2%	+28%	+43%	800-645-6405	NY	1,000
HARTWELL LEVERAGE	+11%	VERY HIGH	− 5%	+27%	+42%	800-645-6405	NY	2,000
ISTEL	+11%	HIGH	− 1%	+11%	+20%	212-702-0174	NY	500
IVY GRTH	+21%	VERY LOW	+ 2%	+16%	+29%	800-235-3322	MA	1,000
JANUS	+18%	LOW	− 4%	+15%	+27%	800-525-3713	CO	1,000
LEGG MASON VAL. TRUST	+24%	LOW	− 3%	+15%	+29%	800-822-5544	MD	1,000
LEHMAN CAPITAL	+18%	MEDIUM	− 6%	+19%	+30%	800-221-5350	NY	1,000
LEHMAN INVESTORS	+18%	MEDIUM	− 2%	+19%	+34%	800-221-5350	NY	500
LEHMAN OPPORTUNITY			− 1%	+13%	NA	800-221-5350	NY	1,000
LEVERAGE FUND BOSTON	+ 9%	VERY HIGH	− 6%	+ 4%	+18%	800-225-6265	MA	1,000
LEXINGTON GRTH	+15%	MEDIUM	− 4%	+23%	+38%	800-526-0056	NJ	1,000
LEXINGTON RESEARCH	+17%	MEDIUM	− 3%	+20%	+36%	800-526-0056	NJ	1,000
LIBERTY AMER. LDRS.	+21%	VERY LOW	+ 1%	+16%	+28%	800-245-4770	PA	500
LOOMIS-SAYLES MUTUAL	+21%	LOW	0%	+29%	+51%	800-223-7124	MA	250
MATHERS	+15%	MEDIUM	0%	+15%	+30%	312-236-8215	IL	1,000
MUTUAL QUAL. INCOME	+22%	VERY LOW	− 4%	+12%	+23%	800-457-0211	MA	1,000
MUTUAL SHARES	+23%	VERY LOW	− 3%	+13%	+23%	800-457-0211	MA	1,000
NATIONAL INDUST.	+ 9%	HIGH	− 5%	+10%	+24%	303-759-2400	CO	250
NEUBERGER—ENERGY		VERY LOW	+ 2%	+ 8%	+16%	800-367-0770	NY	500
NEUBERGER— GUARDIAN	+21%	LOW	+ 5%	+24%	+36%	800-367-0770	NY	500
NEUBERGER— MANHATTAN	+23%	MEDIUM	− 3%	+19%	+37%	800-367-0770	NY	500
NEUBERGER— PARTNERS	+20%	LOW	− 1%	+20%	+34%	800-367-0770	NY	500
NEWTON GRTH	+16%	MEDIUM	0%	+10%	+25%	800-247-7039	WI	1,000
NICHOLAS*	+21%	VERY LOW	− 2%	+14%	+21%	414-272-6133	WI	500
NODDINGS CONVERT. GWTH	+11%	VERY LOW	− 1%	+10%	+15%	800-251-2411	IL	5,000
NODDINGS CONVERT. INCOME	+15%	VERY LOW	− 2%	+14%	+25%	800-251-2411	IL	5,000
NORTH STAR REGIONAL	+19%	LOW	− 4%	+29%	+48%	612-371-7780	MN	2,500
NORTH STAR STOCK	+16%	HIGH	− 3%	+14%	+27%	612-371-7780	MN	1,000

PAST PERFORMANCE

Mutual Funds	One-Year Profit Projection	Risk Rating	Correction 7/4/86–8/22/86	1986 12/31/85–8/22/86	12 Months 8/23/85–8/22/86	Telephone	State	Minimum Initial Investment ($)
NORTHEAST INV. GWTH	+20%	MEDIUM	− 2%	+30%	+51%	800-225-6704	MA	100
NOVA	+12%	HIGH	− 5%	+ 6%	+17%	800-572-0006	MA	2,000
OMEGA	+16%	HIGH	− 2%	+16%	+31%	617-357-8480	MA	1,000
PACIFIC HOR. AGGR. GWTH	+24%	MEDIUM	−11%	+27%	+42%	800-645-3515	CA	1,000
PAX WORLD	+18%	VERY LOW	− 2%	+13%	+26%	603-431-8022	NH	250
PENN SQUARE	+17%	MEDIUM	− 2%	+13%	+28%	800-523-8440	PA	250
PRICE, ROWE, GRTH	+17%	MEDIUM	+ 2%	+25%	+46%	800-638-5660	MD	1,000
PRICE, ROWE, GRTH & INCOME	+15%	LOW	− 1%	+11%	+21%	800-638-5660	MD	1,000
PRICE, ROWE, NEW ERA	+18%	MEDIUM	+ 1%	+15%	+26%	800-638-5660	MD	1,000
PRICE, ROWE, NEW HORIZONS	+13%	HIGH	− 9%	+ 7%	+19%	800-638-5660	MD	1,000
QUEST FOR VALUE			− 3%	+16%	NA	212-825-4000	NY	2,000
RAINBOW	+16%	VERY LOW	− 1%	+18%	+25%	212-509-8532	NY	300
SAFECO EQUITY	+21%	MEDIUM	− 3%	+19%	+35%	800-426-6730	WA	1,000
SAFECO GRTH	+15%	LOW	− 5%	+ 8%	+16%	800-426-6730	WA	1,000
SAFECO INCOME	+23%	VERY LOW	0%	+20%	+33%	800-426-6730	WA	1,000
SCUDDER CAP. GWTH	+19%	LOW	− 4%	+18%	+30%	800-225-2470	MA	1,000
SCUDDER DEVELOPMENT	+12%	HIGH	− 9%	+14%	+23%	800-225-2470	MA	1,000
SCUDDER GWTH & INCOME	+16%	MEDIUM	− 1%	+21%	+37%	800-225-2470	MA	1,000
SELECTED AMER. SHS.	+22%	VERY LOW	− 1%	+21%	+38%	800-621-7321	IL	1,000
SELECTED SPEC. SHS.	+16%	VERY LOW	− 2%	+10%	+20%	800-621-7321	IL	1,000
SMITH BARNEY EQUITY	+17%	MEDIUM	− 3%	+16%	+34%	212-613-2631	NY	100
STATE FARM GRTH	+17%	LOW	− 1%	+14%	+31%	309-766-2029	IL	50
STATE ST. INVEST.*	+17%	MEDIUM	− 1%	+15%	+31%	617-482-3920	MA	0
STEADMAN AMER. INDUS.	− 2%	VERY HIGH	−12%	− 3%	+ 3%	800-424-8570	DC	500
STEADMAN ASSOC.	+12%	HIGH	− 8%	+17%	+33%	800-424-8570	DC	100
STEADMAN INVEST.	+ 3%	VERY HIGH	− 1%	+12%	+ 6%	800-424-8570	DC	500
STEADMAN OCEANOGRA.		VERY HIGH	− 8%	+12%	+11%	800-424-8570	DC	100
STEIN ROE CAPT. OPP.	+13%	VERY HIGH	− 7%	+26%	+41%	800-621-0320	IL	2,500
STEIN ROE DISCOVERY	+12%	HIGH	−13%	+10%	+22%	800-621-0320	IL	2,500
STEIN ROE SPECIAL	+22%	MEDIUM	− 6%	+16%	+28%	800-621-0320	IL	2,500
STEIN ROE STOCK	+15%	HIGH	− 2%	+23%	+35%	800-621-0320	IL	2,500
STEIN ROE TOT. RET.	+16%	VERY LOW	0%	+18%	+29%	800-621-0320	IL	2,500
STEIN ROE UNIVERSE	+12%	HIGH	− 7%	+23%	+33%	800-621-0320	IL	2,500
STRATTON GRTH	+18%	MEDIUM	− 3%	+18%	+30%	215-542-8025	PA	1,000
STRATTON MONTHLY DIV'D	+22%	VERY LOW	+ 6%	+28%	+40%	215-542-8025	PA	1,000
STRONG INVESTMENT†	+19%	VERY LOW	− 1%	+19%	+32%	800-368-3863	WI	250
STRONG TOT. RET.†	+22%	VERY LOW	− 2%	+23%	+39%	800-368-3863	WI	250
20th CENT. GIFT‡	+23%	VERY HIGH	− 9%	+37%	+57%	816-531-5575	MO	100
20th CENT. GROWTH	+19%	VERY HIGH	− 2%	+29%	+49%	816-531-5575	MO	0
20th CENT. SELECT	+24%	HIGH	− 2%	+28%	+47%	816-531-5575	MO	0
20th CENT. ULTRA‡	+16%	VERY HIGH	− 8%	+16%	+30%	816-531-5575	MO	0
20th CENT. VISTA‡	+13%	VERY HIGH	− 9%	+36%	+56%	816-531-5575	MO	0
UNIFIED GRTH	+17%	LOW	− 5%	+16%	+27%	800-862-7283	IN	200
UNIFIED INCOME	+10%	VERY LOW	0%	+ 9%	+13%	800-862-7283	IN	500
UNIFIED MUT. SHARES	+18%	VERY LOW	− 3%	+13%	+27%	800-862-7283	IN	200
UNITED SVS. GOOD-BAD	+14%	LOW	− 4%	+15%	+22%	800-531-5777	TX	500
UNITED SVS. GRTH	+ 2%	VERY LOW	− 7%	+17%	+28%	800-824-4653	TX	500
USAA GRTH	+13%	HIGH	− 6%	+17%	+26%	800-531-8181	TX	1,000
USAA SUNBELT ERA	+13%	HIGH	− 9%	+16%	+22%	800-531-8181	TX	1,000
VALLEY FORGE*	+ 7%	VERY LOW	+ 1%	+ 3%	+ 7%	215-688-6839	PA	2,500
VALUE LINE CONVERT.	+18%	VERY LOW	− 2%	+18%	+29%	800-223-0818	NY	1,000
VALUE LINE FUND	+14%	VERY HIGH	− 4%	+25%	+43%	800-223-0818	NY	1,000

PAST
PERFORMANCE

Mutual Funds	One-Year Profit Projection	Risk Rating	Correction 7/4/86– 8/22/86	1986 12/31/85– 8/22/86	12 Months 8/23/85– 8/22/86	Telephone	State	Minimum Initial Investment ($)
VALUE LINE INCOME	+14%	VERY LOW	− 2%	+19%	+31%	800-223-0818	NY	1,000
VALUE LINE LEV. GWTH	+13%	HIGH	− 3%	+30%	+43%	800-223-0818	NY	1,000
VALUE LINE SPEC. SIT.	+ 8%	VERY HIGH	−10%	+12%	+25%	800-223-0818	NY	1,000
VANGUARD EXP. II	+ 2%	HIGH	− 9%	+ 2%	+10%	800-662-7447	PA	3,000
VANGUARD INDEX	+20%	MEDIUM	0%	+21%	+38%	800-662-7447	PA	1,500
VANGUARD MORG. GWTH	+16%	MEDIUM	− 5%	+10%	+25%	800-662-7447	PA	1,500
VANGUARD NAESS & THOMAS	+10%	HIGH	−12%	+ 9%	+16%	800-662-7447	PA	3,000
VANGUARD STAR	+14%	VERY LOW	0%	+12%	+22%	800-662-7447	PA	500
VANGUARD TCF USA	+16%	MEDIUM	0%	+13%	+23%	800-662-7447	PA	25,000
VANGUARD VSP. SVC. ECON.*	+19%	MEDIUM	− 7%	+19%	+34%	800-662-7447	PA	1,500
VANGUARD WELLESLY INCOME	+22%	VERY LOW	+ 4%	+17%	+30%	800-662-7447	PA	1,500
VANGUARD WELLINGTON	+20%	VERY LOW	+ 1%	+18%	+32%	800-662-7447	PA	1,500
VANGUARD WINDSOR II	+22%	MEDIUM	+ 3%	+25%	+40%	800-662-7447	PA	1,500
VANGUARD WORLD U.S. GR.	+21%	LOW	− 5%	+12%	+31%	800-662-7447	PA	1,500
WEISS PECK GREER TUD*	+20%	HIGH	− 5%	+18%	+32%	800-223-3332	NY	1,000
WEISS PECK GREER WPG	+18%	MEDIUM	− 4%	+17%	+31%	800-223-3332	NY	1,000
WOOD STRU. DE VEGH	+12%	HIGH	− 4%	+14%	+27%	800-221-5672	NY	1,000
WOOD STRU. NEUWIRTH	+18%	MEDIUM	− 9%	+20%	+32%	800-221-5672	NY	1,000
WOOD STRU. PINE ST.	+19%	MEDIUM	− 1%	+18%	+32%	800-221-5672	NY	1,000
ZWEIG FUND			NA	NA	NA	CLOSED-END NYSE		

*1.0% redemption fee
†1.0% sales load
‡0.5% sales load

195

Directory of Income Funds (as of September 5, 1986)

*A*ll funds listed on pages 198–99 accept IRAs and Keoghs and have no sales load or redemption fees. Minimum initial investments are often waived or reduced for IRA, Keogh, and pension accounts. Funds that do not have managed programs for those plans will open accounts for "self-directed" plans.

Mutual Fund	Primary Holding	Yield (%)	Telephone	State	Minimum Initial Investment ($)
AARP GENERAL BOND	CORPORATE	8.0	800-253-2277	MA	250
AARP GNMA	GINNIE MAE	8.8	800-253-2277	MA	250
AXE-HOUGHTON INCOME	CORPORATE	9.0	800-431-1030	NY	1,000
BABSON BOND TRUST	CORPORATE	9.7	800-821-5591	MO	500
BENHAM CAPIT PRES T-NOTE	TREASURY	6.3	800-227-8380	CA	1,000
BENHAM GNMA INCOME	GINNIE MAE	9.9	800-227-8380	CA	1,000
BENHAM TARGET 1990	TREAS—ZERO	6.0	800-227-8380	CA	1,000
BENHAM TARGET 1995	TREAS—ZERO	6.7	800-227-8380	CA	1,000
BENHAM TARGET 2000	TREAS—ZERO	7.4	800-227-8380	CA	1,000
BENHAM TARGET 2005	TREAS—ZERO	7.4	800-227-8380	CA	1,000
BENHAM TARGET 2010	TREAS—ZERO	7.4	800-227-8380	CA	1,000
BULL & BEAR HIGH YIELD	CORPORATE	13.2	800-431-6060	NY	1,000
COLUMBIA FIXED INCOME	GOV. AGENCY	8.6	800-547-1037	OR	1,000
DREYFUS A BONDS PLUS	CORPORATE	8.7	800-645-6561	NY	2,500
DREYFUS GNMA	GINNIE MAE	9.2	800-645-6561	NY	2,500
FIDELITY FLEXIBLE BOND	CORPORATE	9.3	800-544-6666	MA	1,000
FIDELITY GNMA	GINNIE MAE	8.5	800-544-6666	MA	1,000
FIDELITY GOV'T SECURITIES	TREASURY	8.7	800-544-6666	MA	1,000
FIDELITY HIGH INCOME	CORPORATE	11.2	800-544-6666	MA	2,500
FIDELITY MORTGAGE	GOV. AGENCY	9.2	800-544-6666	MA	1,000
FIDELITY THRIFT	CORPORATE	NA	800-544-6666	MA	2,500
FINANCIAL PROG. HIGH YIELD	CORPORATE	11.4	800-525-8085	CO	1,000
GIT MAXIMUM INCOME	CORPORATE	11.1	800-336-3063	VA	1,000
LEXINGTON GNMA INCOME	GINNIE MAE	10.1	800-526-0056	NJ	1,000
LIBERTY U.S. GOV'T SEC.	GOV. AGENCY	9.1	800-245-4770	PA	500
MUTUAL OF OMAHA AMERICA	GOV. AGENCY	8.7	800-228-2499	NE	250

Mutual Fund	Primary Holding	Yield (%)	Telephone	State	Minimum Initial Investment ($)
NEWTON INCOME	CORPORATE	9.2	800-247-7039	WI	1,000
NICHOLAS INCOME	CORPORATE	9.4	414-272-6133	WI	500
NORTHEAST INVESTORS TRUST	CORPORATE	10.3	414-272-6133	WI	500
PRICE, ROWE, HIGH YIELD	CORPORATE	11.1	800-638-5660	MD	1,000
PRICE, ROWE, NEW INCOME	CORPORATE	8.1	800-638-5660	MD	1,000
PRICE, ROWE, SHORT TERM BOND	CORPORATE	7.7	800-638-5660	MD	1,000
PRO INCOME	CORPORATE	7.9	800-523-0864	PA	300
PRUDENTIAL-BACHE ADJ. RATE	PFD. STOCK	7.4	800-872-7787	NY	25,000
PRU-BACHE GOV'T INT.	TREASURY	8.7	800-872-7787	NY	1,000
SCUDDER GOV'T MORTGAGE	GINNIE MAE	8.9	800-225-2470	MA	1,000
SCUDDER INCOME	CORPORATE	9.4	800-225-2470	MA	1,000
20th CENTURY U.S. GOV'T	TREASURY	8.1	816-531-5575	MO	0
USAA INCOME	GOV. AGENCY	9.3	800-531-8181	TX	1,000
VALUE LINE U.S. GOV'T	GINNIE MAE	9.9	800-223-0818	NY	1,000
VANGUARD FI. HIGH YIELD	CORPORATE	11.3	800-662-7447	PA	3,000
VANGUARD FI. INVST GRADE	CORPORATE	9.8	800-662-7447	PA	3,000
VANGUARD FI. SHORT TERM	CORPORATE	8.1	800-662-7447	PA	3,000
VANGUARD FIX. INCOME GNMA	GINNIE MAE	9.8	800-662-7447	PA	3,000
VANGUARD QUALIF. DIV'D III	PFD. STOCK	6.9	800-662-7447	PA	25,000
VANGUARD QUALIF. DIV'D II	PFD. STOCK	9.0	800-662-7447	PA	1,500

Note: Income fund information is provided courtesy of *Income & Safety*, 3471 N. Federal Highway, Fort Lauderdale, Florida 33306. A free copy of the publication is available.

INDEX

Advertisements for IRA
   investments, 33–36, 75–76
Age:
   to begin withdrawals from
      IRAs, 46–50, 56, 187
   choice of investment vehicles
      and, 55
   eligibility to open an IRA and,
      38, 46
   at initial investment in an IRA,
      xiii–xvi, 39–41
Aggressive growth funds, 62–63
Alimony, 41, 185
Annuities, 50, 180
   borrowing on an annuity
      contract, 189
   income from, 41
   IRAs invested in, 18, 51, 66, 176
Automatic transfer of funds to
      IRA from checking account,
      186
Avatar Associates, 20, 21

Balanced funds, 63–64
Bank certificates of deposit, 65
   see also Certificates of deposit
      (CDs)
Bankers' acceptances, 65
Banks, investment of funds with,
      56–58, 61, 62
Barron's, 21, 118, 119, 144, 152
Bernhard & Co., Arnold, 111
Bond Fund Timer, 118

Bond market, 9, 143–44
Bonds, 64, 65
   average long-term yield of, 78–
      80, 91, 92–93, 100–101, 177
   buy-and-hold approach to, 148,
      149, 150, 151, 154, 161
   diversifying holdings, 182
   inflation's effect on yields of, 93–
      94, 96–100
   interest on, 91
   investing IRAs in, 18, 91–101
   model for trading, see Model for
      trading bond mutual funds
   risk of, 91, 100, 169, 177–78
   tax-exempt, 58, 188
   U.S. Government, 77–81, 91, 93,
      144, 172–75, 182
   zero coupon, 64, 94–99, 172–75,
      178
   see also Mutual funds
Borrowing:
   on an annuity contract, 189
   to finance an IRA contribution,
      182–83
   from an IRA, 185, 188–89
Brazil, 88–89
Business Timing Guide, 118
Buy-and-hold approach, 178
   to bonds, 148, 149, 150, 151, 154,
      161
   to stocks, 19, 20, 114, 116, 126,
      139–42
Buyout activity, stock market, 5

201